Amy and Dave's Glacier Escape Tour – 2025

David Stoeckl

Amy & Dave's Glacier Escape Tour – 2025
Copyright ©2025 by David Stoeckl. All rights reserved.

Published by David Stoeckl and Albedo Books, Sequim, WA 98382
Albedobooks@gmail.com

All rights reserved. No part of this publication may be reproduced, stored in a retrieval system or transmitted in any form by any means, electronic, mechanical, photocopy, recording, computer scanned, or otherwise, without the prior permission of the publisher, except as provided by USA copyright law.

Cover photo and book design by: David Stoeckl
Released October, 2025

ISBN 978-1-967695-10-2 – eBook
ISBN 978-1-967695-14-0 – Printed Book

*** This book composed and produced **without** assistance from **AI**.

**To Emi, my niece,
who added her bits
and tidbits of life
throughout the book**

Introduction – Before We Left
Earlier July, 2025

Sometimes people do things because someone else wants to do them. Has that happened to you? Most likely.

In the spring of 2025, my wife, Amy, received a call from her sister, Carrie who lives near Omaha, NE. Carrie and her husband, Nate, are both Air Force officers – Carrie a Major, and Nate a Lieutenant Colonel. Nate is planning to retire soon, just for the record.

They planned a summer trip to Yellowstone National Park in Wyoming and invited us to join them. That did not work out. But, then they planned to head north to Glacier National Park in Montana. The timing was far more favorable for our lives, so we planned to join them.

We have an old 31' Tiffin Allegro motorhome which we've christened the name Morris. You can read about our first big trip in Morris in Amy & Dave's COVID Escape Tour – 2021. We had not taken Morris for a longer trip since 2021. Long overdue.

Montana would be the perfect week long adventure to enjoy some RV camping.

To be honest, I did very little of the planning. Amy and Carrie set the dates. Amy found and reserved days at the Mountain Meadows RV Campsite near Columbia Falls, MT. Any camping sites in Glacier National Park were long ago reserved.

We were blessed to find space at Mountain Meadows.

Neither Amy nor I had visited Glacier, so BIG attraction to see it. We'd both camped at Yellowstone and the Grand Tetons, so Glacier seemed like a sweet trip to see this summer.

As plans developed, Amy offered for Carrie, Nate and their 9-year-old daughter, Emi to stay with us at the campsite. They called each other regularly over the weeks before the trip to plan activities. Nate and I kinda just became the drivers, at least until we got there.

I made sure Morris was prepped for the trip. It visited the local RV repair shop for a once through. Nothing big. For a 35 year old RV, it still seems to love to run and get us wherever we want to go.

I guess that's all I need to say about getting ready for the trip, who would be there, and let the following pages share with you how the trip evolved and became sweet history.

PS - The pics are all in Black and White, so I focused more on people than landscape. Ansel Adams would have appreciated the need to get such landscape pics perfect.

Monday, July 7, 2025
Heading Out

We had planned to get out of town by 9 a.m. that morning, but that did not happen. We had spent way too much time working on the yard, (and house) the previous few days. Amy wanted to pressure-wash the world. Starting with the back deck, we pulled everything off – plants, furniture, etc. Everything except the inflatable hot tub and barbecue, then pressure washed it. We even pressure washed the 10'X7' jute rug which had become quite green in places. It looked significantly better after the pressure washer.

Then, she continued down the sidewalk. I completed the sidewalk. The next day, she pressure-washed the oval patio where we have our portable fire pit, and/or fire ring. Later, we pressure-washed the front porch and sidewalk to the driveway. The leaf blower also made itself useful. Amy weeded a bunch of the front driveway and such – a whole bunch of work that looked great but created a terrible cost in time, money and energy.

Even after I pressure-washed the sidewalk, I took the pressure washer to our RV which had not been washed since we'd owned it. It was FILTHY, on the back and driver side. The difference was truly remarkable. The passenger side and the front looked a bit better, not nearly so soiled. The driver side lives in the shade beside the trees, so the perfect environment for green schtuff to collect. I didn't do the roof, but the RV looked much, much better after getting pressure-washed. Yay!

A few days earlier, Amy had completed crocheting a handbag. It had been awhile since she'd crocheted. Maybe her tendons were not ready for such a task because her thumbs on both hands responded painfully. One thumb would click over and over as she moved it. The other, the tendon area pressed against the skin of her hand by the wrist. Lots of pain. She had to wear braces or tape the thumbs when she wasn't treating them with ice. The very physical yardwork totally added to the discomfort.

So, the day before our trip, we were more than busy getting the house cleaned up as I loaded our old 1990 Tiffin Allegro RV.

Amy later admitted she seemed to want to pack like we did for our month and a half long trek in 2021. I composed Amy and Dave's COVID Escape

Tour - 2021. This one will be Amy and Dave's Glacier Escape Tour - 2025.

Before the sixth, I had cleaned out much of the RV, and went through the cupboards, both cleaning out things we would not want to take as well as taking inventory of what still could be used for this trip. Things like paper plates, cups, cooking utensils, kitchen towels and cleaning supplies were totally at home in the old RV. I was more than amused when I found a few Hershey chocolates on the bottom of one of the food cupboards from 2021. Those were not going to make this trip, and enjoyed their last great hurrah to the garbage can.

I also wiped down everything with Clorox wipes and made lists of things I wanted to take with us. I'm a list maker for most of my trips. It helps me not forget things. It's not perfect, but it definitely helps. I kept the list on the kitchen counter the week before our trip to refer to as well as add anything else.

So, Monday morning, July 7th, 2025, we still had a BUNCH of stuff to load to get ready for the trip. We also finished cleaning up the house, running the dishwasher and Swiffering floors. I did a load of laundry, just 'cuz. I have another trip helping people move out of state, as soon as I get back, so getting all my laundry done before I'm gone for another week is a blessing of preparation.

Each hour we thought would be our last. Amy's sister, Carrie, called around 9:30. Amy said we'd be gone by 10. I said, "11." Nope. Didn't make that time, either, though our striving efforts were truly admirable.

We had a few other preparations before our big day. Old Morris had not been driven very far for the last couple of years or so. As I said in my last travel book, RV's have a strange life. They sit for months – even years in the driveway, then are expected to drive 2,000 miles. We took a trip with our two Australian Shepherds to Port Angeles and beyond. Not a BIG trip, at all, but definitely long enough to note any immediate problems.

Our last trip, the passenger wiper was getting more than worn and useless. I tried to replace it, but nobody has those old wipers anywhere. I've checked Campers World and other RV places, as well as online and cannot find them. I have done a preliminary check to just replace the entire wiper arm, but I don't think the mechanism will fit the present wiper arms. Maybe I'm wrong.

What I did instead was clean it with Rainex. That schtuff is amazing. It's middle of summer and good chance we'll see zero rain, but if we do, the rain should bead on the windshield, keeping my vision of the road totally safe. I also tried something else, wiping WD-40 on both blades. They were both a bit crusty, so wiped clean and the WD-40 will keep them a bit softer and smoother if needed, (hopefully).

Finally loaded, we were able to get out of the driveway around 12:30.

I mentioned our 2 Aussies. We love our dogs and truly wanted to bring them with us, but US national parks do not allow dogs on the trails. We discussed the dogs extensively with Amy's sister, Carrie, who is kenneling her two aussies for their family vacation. We did not want to kennel them, partially because of the price. It's a significant expense to kennel your dogs now. Almost as much as Motel 6 for the night.

Fortunately, we met a very nice young woman named Shelby who had moved into the area recently. She was good friends with our son's closest Sequim friend. He talked to her and she contacted us. We enjoyed meeting her and taking the dogs for walks while she was with us three different occasions. One of our aussies is a bit skittish, so having her meet and walk her before we left was not a luxury or in any way frivolous. She was also more than willing to stay in our home for less than half the cost of the kennel. What a bargain. Better quality care for half the cost. The dogs would get to remain home where they were most comfortable. What a blessing. Thank You, Jesus.

Shelby also works from home doing sales and marketing, so could work out of our home just as easily. She has a small dog named Loki who totally got along with our younger dog, Toby. They played like old friends from the start. Our other dog, Cricket, is only 6, but as I said, more skittish. She lived in a kennel as a breeder dog before we got her this year, so she never learned to play with other dogs. She's a sweety and LOVES to be petted and loved. It's sad in many ways that such a critter lived this solitary life until she no longer produced litters. She had to learn to live in a family home, walk down the street with cars and trucks and kids and whatever passing by. It took a bit to get her used to the changes. She's still a bit nervous, but coming along better and better each month. We'll see how she does when we get back from this trip.

Amy and I took a brief trip in January, just 20 days after we got her. She did not do well with our absence, but she was still very new to the changes. We expected she would do much better this time.

Still, we were not very far down the road when I said to Amy I still wished we'd brought the dogs. We could have left them in the RV when we went to Glacier, but feared the AC would stop working while we were gone for the day, killing our dogs. Not that our AC ever quit working, but in the summer, one dares not take any chances. As much as we wanted them with us, we adjudged the best decision dictated we leave them home. Sitting in Morris on our first day of travel, I miss them a bunch as I write.

Okay, so now we're on our way. "On the road again..."

Not so fast!

We had to stop at Safeway and get firewood, ice and something else I could not remember until after we left. Not far from Safeway, I said to Amy, "Big bottles of water! Whyizit we always forget something we have to get if we don't write it down?"

We didn't go back. We don't drink the water in the fresh water tank of the RV. It's fine for washing hands and dishes because we have lots of soap, but I don't trust drinking it. The bottled water is critical. We had 40 packs of small bottles, but the gallons have a fair amount of convenience, for drinking, coffee, (which is also drinking) and cooking. We would get some later.

Sooooo, NOW we finally can hit the road.

Nope. Amy hosted a tea social a month or so back and had to return one of the fancy, old teapots she'd borrowed. 30+ women attended. The gala social affair of the year at hour church. WooWoo! But, we wanted to drop off the teapot with our friend, Sandy, before we left. Her son and boyfriend also got to see Morris in all his travel glory. He looked so much better after being pressure washed.

Amusingly, neither of the men mentioned a couple flat 4X4 boards I'd stored in the living room area behind the couch. They rise up well above the back of the couch, mostly covering the window. And, why did we feel the need to bring a couple 4X4 flat boards on a camping trip? So, Amy could practice her tap dancing. She'd been doing tap dancing for the last couple years, even performing with her dance instructor and fellow students in two dance reviews in Sequim. Much fun.

She even brought her first pair of tap shoes to give to her niece, Emi, whom we'll see at Glacier National Park.

Soooooo, now that we've dropped off the critically important teapot, we finally got on the road around 1:30. Our first destination: Fruitland, WA - around 70 miles east of Spokane. The GPS says it takes around $6\frac{1}{2}$ hours to drive to this little, unincorporated township where my brother Jay and his wife Jennifer live. Driving a 35-year-old, 33' Class A Motorhome with a 5.9L Cummins Diesel ain't gonna make any trip anywhere as fast as the GPS says.

Most trips, I trim off a few of the minutes from GPSville. With Morris, I easily knew to add an hour, if not more.

One thing about Morris is that it doesn't like uphills very well. The radiator and water pump and all seem to be fine, but the temp gage often moves up to the top of the red zone on many of the hills. It's never boiled over.

After our little Port Angeles trip two days earlier, I checked the coolant level. Right up to the tiptop of the radiator. The overflow was full of coolant. I touched the radiator shortly after we got home. It was warm, but nowhere nearly as hot as I would expect any vehicle which threatens to boil over any second.

Along the regular roads, the gage is fine. It's only the longer uphills that jump up. As soon as we reach the top, the needle readily moves back down to the green zone.

Our last trip, we had to drive over Snoqualmie Pass, east of Seattle. This hot day, we had to traverse the same long uphill pass.

Oddly, we took Highway 18, near Auburn, WA. It had a small uphill section that Morris read dangerously HOT, but it got over that and rapidly cooled down. So, I expect more of the same for way too long heading over Snoqualmie. To my pleasant surprise, Snoqualmie was cake. I took time, not pressing down on the accelerator for max speed. Just take time and get up the hill with the semis, flashers flashing.

Amy got a call from her son, Kyler. Near the top of the pass, I gave her a thumbs up. All was fine and we kept driving in the not-too-hot zone the rest of the trip.

The drive to little Fruitland is a nice trip. We've made the trip a couple/3 times previously, so familiar landmarks this time around. You stay on I-90 eastbound well past Ellensburg, WA. We ignored the turn off towards Yakima, continuing along 90.

The biggest concern of driving Morris on the interstate comes when some of the semis pass, blowing us to the right. Our Big Box does not have much weight to volume ratio so side winds can change its direction a little too easily. I readily correct, but it's always a bit of a head rush concern while driving.

The driver's seat is also not nearly as comfortable as I'd like. It always makes me feel like it's leaning inward towards the middle of the vehicle - not good for my back and quickly uncomfortable within the first hour of driving.

This time, I tried putting other cushiony items on the plush seat to position me a bit taller and see if it was more comfortable. It was a bit better, but I still had to adjust position every few minutes or so the entire trip.

Our only stop along the way - the Ryegrass Rest Area, just past Ellensburg. We had stopped here before one time - don't ask me when. I'll probably remember, but really don't want to work that hard; mostly because it does not matter.

I just needed a bit of time to stretch my legs. The facilities were appreciated as well, though the urinal was apparently clogged and the water wouldn't shut-off. It ran and ran over, washing down the floor drain. I tried pushing the flush button again to entice the urinal to quick running. No go. I came back a bit later, and by that time it got the need to perpetually flush out of its system, at least for the moment. Amy and I took a couple pics there. It was warm and breezy, and felt absolutely wonderful after our chillier days in Sequim. We call it Junuary, and this year could have been Julyary with temps rarely reaching 70 before we left.

One of the funnest towns in Washington state is called George. George, Washington. How fun is that?

They used to have a very large bust of our first president near the freeway. I looked for it, but did not see it. Maybe it is still there, but I could not see it.

The first time I saw it was when I was a 17-year-old vagabond hitchhiker. I got a ride to George and was surprised to see the bust of old George, bigger than life. So, I always look for it, but I think it's been either moved or permanently retired.

For our trip, that's where we change roads, leaving I-90 to head north towards Grand Coolee Dam. Just to cover the pathways, you leave I-90 at George, taking Highway 283 North. Around Naylor, it turns into Highway 28 to Soap Lake where it turns into Highway 17. You're still heading north towards Coolee City. Not many miles from Grand Coolee Dam, (which we never actually see), you turn right onto Highway 2 Eastbound, to the town of Creston. Just past town, the roads we need stop being highway numbers. We turned left onto Miles Creston Road N which we enjoyed for 19 miles. Then, left on Creston Road which is also Highway 25 for the last 16 miles to Fruitland.

Along this route, the terrain turns into farmland, similar to the farm where Amy grew up in northeastern Colorado. One previous trip, Amy took a pic and sent it to her sister, asking where she thought that was. She answered, "Colorado or Nebraska." Nope. Central Washington.

Completing the day's drive, my brother Jay, and Jennifer live just due south of beautiful downtown Fruitland on a 28-acre chunk of land. They have a booming business called the Dire Wolf Project which Jenn has run for decades. These huge, lovable dogs are amazing, gentle giants. Nothing not to love about them. Jenn makes YouTube videos weekly, showing the latest litters, developing and training the dogs to be your perfect companion.

We had hoped to be there by 5 pm. We got there shortly after 9, just before dark. Jenn met us outside and directed us to Morris' best parking spot by a couple new kennels that were not there last time we were here. One of those kennels had momma dog with her brood of eight fun-loving puppies.

My brother Jay was gone on a driving job in Seattle - something he does, not often, but regularly. They called for him last week. He accepted the job then found it would be while we were here.

No worries. Jay's my closest sibling, so in that way we'll miss his company, but Amy and Jenn will talk away the hours, giving me time to write this book. We can still play guitar and visit with the doggies and eat more food than we need to eat and so on.

Jenn visited till after midnight, then headed to bed. Just boring talking schtuff. Perfect. Thereafter, Amy rested on the bed while I checked computer and phone schtuff I had not been able to attend to because of the demands of traveling. Finally, around 2 a.m., we turned out the lights for the night.

Our Onan generator went belly-up since our last trip. I tried to replace it, and had a friend named Hugh who's great with small engines, try to fix it. He determined that the problem was electrical. He checked the voltage regulator and tested the small circuit board, even re-soldering some of the connections.

The difference?

Before, it would turn over and over without a spark of life.

Now it turns over and starts but immediately stalls when we take fingers off the starter.

With the generator not working and unable to find a suitable replacement, (our Onan runs on propane, not gasoline – a much less common generator), we decided to get another regular, dual fuel portable generator. It would ride on a cargo carrier, hanging off the Class C hitch. Last week, we found this homemade cargo carrier in Port Angeles for only fifty bucks. It's totally heavy duty and more than enough to carry a generator and 5-gallon propane tank. I stood on it while pressure washing Morris.

Unfortunately, the guy who made it gave it an extra long tongue so he could open his truck tailgate. Being extra long, it takes very little for it to scrape on the road when entering driveways and such. We had to find a Class C hitch thingy that raised up the cargo carrier a few inches. That took care of the scraping problem.

We made it all the way to Fruitland without a mishap, then scraped a bunch when we turned into Jay & Jenn's very rustic property. On the way, our other stop found Harbor Freight in Silverdale, WA, who had two such metal pieces that would do the trick. I got the more heavy duty one. We planned to change it out tomorrow.

We're well practiced wimps when it comes to temperatures in the 90's or higher. The generator would certainly earn its keep its first day of usage.

Amy and Morris at the Rest Area

Tuesday, July 8, 2025
Fruitland, WA

    I'm a person who does not need 8 hours of sleep a night. Actually, if I get 8 hours or more, I awaken groggy - a condition I often cannot shake the rest of the day. Though we found our bed after 2 a.m. last night, I was glad to rise around 7:30.

    Our bed is in the back of the RV. The generator ran all night, keeping the RV cool, not just with the AC, but also we like to sleep with a fan blowing. Online says a 5 gallon tank will last around 12 hours run time on half load. I had not topped off the tank before we left, yet it ran all night and well into the morning.

    I have not yet mentioned Henry. Henry is one of Jenn's Dire Wolves, full grown, who was not taken care of very well. So, after some aggressive discussions, Henry was reunited with Jay and Jenn. He's not being used as a breeder, but he's also not being kept in the kennels. He has free reign around the property and loves to see what you're doing. He's also always looking for a handout - ie, some loving affection.

    Like I said, Jenn's Dire Wolves are, well, not wolves at all. Many resemble wolves, yet these very large dogs have a sweet disposition that is amazingly friendly. Even docile. They love everyone, and Jenn takes time to train them to be the perfect animal to any and all who get one of their dogs.

Even more impressive, they deliver the dogs to the buyers anywhere in the continental US. Jay has taken up to 8 dogs (that I know of) to destinations across America. The load of 8 had three adults and 5 puppies.

When someone gets a puppy, Jay basically makes sure the home looks appropriate for the dog. He might be there 15 minutes or so – not long. But, when he brings an adult dog, these dogs have grown up with Jay & Jenn, so that's their people. Jay takes whatever time it takes to get the dog a bit used to its new home before he leaves.

He even related one story where the new owners in Massachusetts took their dog to the dog park its second day with them. It got spooked by something and took off. They could not find her, and she had not had sufficient time to totally bond with the new owners.

They called Jay and reported what had happened. He was in Ohio at the time, so turned around and went back to Massachusetts. He stayed in and around his car watching for the dog. He eventually found her, and she promptly and happily came to him. He stayed with the dog and new owners some hours before heading out again.

Jay is very levelheaded. He did not get all in a tight wad about what happened. He felt more glad that he'd found their beautiful dog and could help share the happy ending. Of course, today the dog loves its new home and is well bonded with the owners.

One time, a couple in Yachats, OR bought one of their dogs. Jay delivered it. A month or so later, she was re-diagnosed with lung cancer. The therapy would take her away from being able to property care for the female. Jay was on another run, delivering dogs, so called me and asked us to pick-up the sweet girl. We were glad to go, took the drive to the beautiful Oregon coast, and met these mildly eccentric, very likable people.

They had tried running a bed and breakfast, but the customers were often irritating. She told me one called her at 2 in the morning complaining it was too damp for them to sleep. Hey! You're on the Oregon coast by some big body of water called the Pacific Ocean. What did you expect?

We were blessed to stay in their large and lovely bed and breakfast room with a loft bedroom.

What a blessing. The next day, we visited with them for an hour or more, sharing life and getting the dog loaded in the crate. Amy's Kia Soul could barely contain the large transport kennel.

We took the dog home and a few days later, met Jay in Seattle, heading home from his dog deliveries. Amy's youngest daughter wanted to keep her. (We love the dogs, but do not have a sufficiently large back yard for such a magnificent animal).

We enjoyed dinner out with my brother, and transferred the doggie to his minivan. There's a part of me that still wishes we could have kept her. So, today we spent a very warm day mostly inside, protected by the AC. I got to read my Bible this morning with a cup of coffee. I was reading the Book of Daniel. Amy eventually arose, had her coffee, then took time to do a bunch of organization on our living quarters. Getting in later last night and visiting with Jenn, we kind of had to find our way around, trying to remember where I put things, and find things like charging cords. The RV was a bit of a mess and was much more ready to receive visitors today.

Jenn surprised us with breakfast. Amy added melon and strawberries and more. We visited in our RV while dining.

More food. More visiting. Then, Amy and Jenn decided it was nap time. I worked a couple book puzzles, then started working on this book some more.

In the evening, we pulled out boneless pork chops. We'd brought some frozen items, but our poor, old RV fridge just does not cool like it should anymore. It cools, but the freezer doesn't freeze until it's consistently plugged in for some days. It runs on either electricity, when plugged-in, or the generator, or it runs off of onboard propane.

I checked the back of the fridge. No flame that I could see so the propane system likely was not working. I fired up the generator which would eventually cool the fridge and save our food. At that time, the ice chest worked more efficiently.

I checked ChapGPT for solutions. I learned a bit, but I am pretty sure none of it will help much before we get back. I expect the fridge, which is original equipment – 35 years old, has lived its useful life and needs to be replaced. TBD. It's over a grand for a new fridge. If we decide to keep Morris, it will be worth the investment. Again, TBD.

When we get to the RV site at Glacier National Park, I expect that we'll be able to keep it plugged all day and night, so the fridge will work the whole time. Right now, if the generator is not on, the fridge is not cooling. Amy tossed a bag of ice in the freezer. It helped keep things cool – obviously not frozen, and the ice melted, making a wet mess to have to sop up in the bottom of the small freezer. You'd think the makers of ice bags would make them watertight.

The moving hum of the generator is actually somewhat soothing. We left it on all night our first night, and slept very well. It reminded me a bit of when we were on our COVID Escape Tour in 2021. One night, we parked next to a semi in Wright, WY. It kept its engine on all night – I have no idea why, but the sound was actually comforting to me to sleep beside.

I don't like sleeping, anyway. If I never had to sleep, (and could function), a part of me would revel. It's not like I am super-efficient and productive throughout all of my waking hours. I'm not, but there's a part of my brain that still hates to give up that many hours of my life to nothing productive, (other than giving the body a rest to be able to function the next day).

Starting the generator also gave me a cup of coffee. That can certainly make the morning a better place. We brought along our Keurig coffee maker. Amy LOVES her morning coffee. I'm guessing we won't need the generator much after we get to Glacier.

Before noon, we piled into Jenn's minivan to head to town. "Town" is a relative term. Fruitland, WA really is just a wide spot along the narrow highway. It has a small gas station and store – really the only business one notices. Besides scant grocery options, they have propane and ice and other camping schtuff. We refilled our propane tanks and got a few probably unneeded food items. Back at the J&J homestead, I happily helped Jenn water the dogs. They are all so happy for the attention. It's really fun to engage with them.

Amy went to lay down and discovered the rug in the bedroom was very wet. We checked for where the water might have come from. Nothing showed leaking, so we sopped up what we could, and pointed a fan to help dry it before it mildewed.

That evening, we barbecued the pork chops. Jenn had an 8 pack of corn from Costco, pre-shucked. Amy cooked those in a watery, buttery pan, also on the barbecue. Yum! There's a part of me that would have been completely happy just to eat corn for dinner.

Jenn also got some sort of salad kit. I liked it a bunch. Amy had some, but cannot eat much ruffage, and Jenn is on a special diet right now, so could not have any of the salad.

Just before dinner, I started a campfire. After dinner and preliminary clean-up, we got out my guitar and Amy's cajon to play some music between chats and such. It's still funny to me how most of us eventually turn into old folks who are happy to sit and jaw for hours.

We brought a propane fire ring with rocks, but opted for the wood fire. The ring keeps things a bit cleaner. There's not a lot of smoke flowing one way or another while you're sitting around it. It shuts off and can be moved within minutes to wherever you might want to keep it or use it again. Perhaps best of all, you don't wake up the next day smelling like smoke.

On the other hand, cooking a hot dog over a woodfire honestly tastes better. I made some over the propane ring last week. They were okay, but clearly not as tasty.

Jenn said the mosquitoes have been few and far between this year. I always seem to attract them. I got a bite on my leg the first night, and another on the same leg the second night, by the fire. We'd brought Off!, so I doused myself.

The BIG buggy attraction there are the moths. Dozens and dozens of the critters, flying all around and on us. They're not bad like mosquitoes or wasps, of course, but a bit obnoxious when you're sitting there. Judging by their attractions to us, they must love the light of Christ within us.

After midnight, we headed back to our quarters. I stayed up for a spell before heading to sleep. It was quite a bit cooler than the first night. Amy had become a bit chilled by the fire, so had a hard time getting warm enough to sleep. She added 2 more small blankets to sleep under. I was fine with just the sheet and blanket.

When we got Morris, it had a sponge rubber mattress with cut-off corners at the foot of the bed. This allowed access to each side of the bedroom, but it also made the bed shorter – a bit too short for this tall person. We swapped it out for a regular queen-sized mattress. We have to climb over the mattress to get to either side of the bed, but it's much more comfortable to sleep on.

A few years back, Amy and I decided to change our king-sized bed for a queen size – to make a little more room in our home bedroom. Amy never quite got comfortable with it. It always felt to her like the bed was too narrow. After one short month, she bought a California King – a little less wide than a regular king, but 3 inches longer for my lengthy stretches when lying down.

I would have expected similar response sleeping on the queen sized bed in Morris, but it never seems quite so cramped at all. Despite the smaller width of the queen-sized bed in Morris, I think it's more than comfortable sleeping side-by-side.

Having bought the queen-sized bed new for our bedroom, we sold it for a considerable loss. Then, a month or two later, daughter Quinnlyn moved out. She took her bed. We could have placed the almost new Queen in her room, but it was already long gone. C'est la vie.

Bedding down for the night in Morris, I got to write a little more before heading to bed. We ended up not changing out the Class C hitch to raise up the cargo holder. Tomorrow is soon enough, just so long as we change it before we have to leave on Thursday.

Wednesday, July 9, 2025
One More Day in Fruitland

We really needed a shower. Morris has a shower and a little 7-gallon propane water heater. We also saw the little store in town had showers for ten bucks. One way or another, we we're going to get the grime of these 2 wonderful days off our bods before we headed to Glacier.

Amy made the reservation for the RV park near Glacier. I saw it had showers but felt too grungy to wait until tomorrow. It's remarkable how much better one feels after getting cleaned up, so I warmed up the water tank and took a quick shower. What a blessing!

Before it got too hot, we took the generator off the cargo carrier to raise it up with the Class C hitch adapter we'd bought in Silverdale. Some lifting and hefting and being careful, but it actually all went together pretty easily. I installed the adapter on the cargo carrier first, then fit it into the Class C hitch on Morris. I thought the lower height would be easier to install the cargo carrier. (I didn't try it both ways to see if I was right.)

Suddenly, a problem presented itself I apparently did not foresee when I bought the adapter. When you install something into a Class C hitch, you lock it in with a small, metal rod, perfectly sized for the hitch. An even smaller, springy piece of metal locks that rod into place. Buying the hitch adapter, I now needed 2 of the metal rods and springy locks. Don't you LOVE feeling like a fool when you shoulda known better?

We had emptied yesterday's 5-gallon LP tank on the generator, so went back to the Fruitland gas station/convenience store we'd visited yesterday and got more fuel, more ice and snacks. Fortunately, they also had the rod and lock I needed in their little, overpacked shop. I would not have been able to leave Fruitland with the raised hitch without the rod and lock.

Yesterday, as I was wandering through the store, I even commented on how efficiently they fit a whole lot of merchandise into a small space. We were blessed they had a small, small section for tow-hitch needs. My rod and lock were available. I'm sure it would have been cheaper at Harbor Freight, but at that moment I didn't care.

Returning to J&J's, we finished installing the raised cargo carrier. Amy and I got the heavy generator onto it without much trouble at all. Practice makes perfect, I guess.

We made a tentative plan to meet up with J&J on the way back from Glacier since he was gone this visit. They'll come down to I-90 to get together with us for a meal. Jenn offered to lend us another 5-gallon propane bottle. (We had another one at home. I should've known to bring it). We can return it when we see them on the way back. Very sweet of her.

Last night, Amy ate a premixed salad Jenn had gotten at Costco in Spokane. It had cabbage in it – something Amy has had problems eating, especially if it's raw. She tried just a little, but it caused her gut to be in knots much of the night. She didn't sleep well and had to move out onto the couch where she could more easily sleep less horizontally.

At her request, I texted Jenn around 7:30 to Not bring breakfast like the day before. Fruitland is very remote, and phone calls, texts, etc. do not like to make the trek across the cosmos. She never received my message – a fact I noticed later after she brought nicely seasoned scrambled eggs covered with cheese to our RV. Fortunately, eggs set well with Amy's stomach, so it turned out to be one of the best breakfasts she could have selected.

As we planned the rest of our last day here, Jenn brought over some chicken salad and potato salad she'd gotten from afore mentioned Costco. The women snacked on rice cake chips as we played a card game called Guillotine. It's called Guillotine, but the head chopper has nothing to do with the game at all. It's given an 18th century France theme with King Louie XVI and Marie Antoinette. Both monarchs died by the guillotine, so I guess that makes the game more authentic somehow.

Anyway, I've only played the game a few times, but as yet I've not won. Amy and I had only played against each other. Fun to have a third player. Amy took the first game. Jenn the second. I was tail's-cow both games. I'm glad I don't have to have my head chopped off for losing yet again.
After that, it was O-Nap-Thirty, as Amy calls it. Jenn and Amy took a sweet rest away from the heat and I got to do a little typing for this journal-like book.

One of the most remarkable things about Fruitland is the Emerson family. I mentioned them in Amy & Dave's COVID Escape Tour – 2021. Well-established folks in this very small town with lots of land, they invested in their sons. Donnie, the second oldest, is a natural born musician, composer, singer, etc. Their dad put together a recording studio on the property. Donnie and his brother Joe put together an amazing album called Dreamin' Wild, around 1979.

Of course, it never sold. No distribution. No radio airtime. However good it was, it was doomed to fail.

Then, a collector found the album years later and wanted to re-release it with a legitimate distribution platform. It did fine. Its main song, Baby, got lots of air play and used in a few movies. The remarkable story became enshrined in its own feature length motion picture, also called Dreamin' Wild. Casey Affleck plays Donnie and Zooey Deschanel plays his wife.

We'd met the family 2 previous trips. I also worked with Donnie in Spokane in 2024, recording music in a studio. We wanted to visit the Emersons again, but they were not available today. We're on our way tomorrow for Glacier, so (sadly) we would not be able to be reacquainted.

In the Dreamin' Wild movie, they showed a nighttime shot of beautiful downtown Fruitland. As yet, I had not seen it. In fact, until I saw the movie, I thought the wide spot in the road where we got gas and snacks was the core of the community. We chatted about that with Jenn, and I discovered that the "wide spot" in the road really was beautiful downtown Fruitland - ie, there isn't one. The final shot in the movie that makes it look particularly quaint and attractive, is actually another small town, called Hunters, some miles north of Fruitland.

Hunters.

That sounds like a great name for a community in the sticks where hunting and fishing are supreme.

Beautiful downtown Hunters ain't much to look at, either. It has a post office, very small grocery store and the bar next door. That's the bar used in the Dreamin' Wild movie. They have the movie poster on the wall as you walk in.

I have to back up a bit. During our two visits to the gas station/convenience store in Fruitland, a lone man sat outside both times. He wore the same black shirt each day. He started his day with a Coors Light. We greeted him each time. Now this day, during the afternoon, walking into the Hunters Bar, there he was, still sporting that same black T-shirt. We greeted each other again and joked about stalking one another.

There's nothing fancy about the bar. It has a long wooden bar, almost the length of the main room. 6 taller tables with stools. I watched the Mariners game broadcast over the lone TV, playing against the Yankees who swept the series while we were there. Heading further in, there's a small but decent stage for music. That's where Donnie and Joe played their final songs of the movie.

As a last mention of Donnie Emerson, in the summer of 2024, I was blessed to hire him to record as many of my musical compositions as we could record in five days. Just me and my guitar in the Spokane, WA studio. We got about 30 songs done. Only 60-70 left to record after I got home. My music never went anywhere, like my books, so it's another something to leave to my kids.

He's a totally focused producer, and I'm happy with the quality of the recordings. We also got to talk about Dreamin' Wild a bit.
Back to Hunters, WA bar.

The back room has 2 pool tables – one regular and one coin operated. Honestly, it was delightful to see a real pool table that one did not have to pay to play, (other than food or drink). We turned on the pool room lights and played a couple games – me against the 2 women.

I'm only slightly embarrassed to say it wasn't pretty. I've never been like a decent pool player at any time of my life, and I've played maybe twice in the last decade, but I still did not expect me to be that bad. Use it or lose it.

I won both games. This is only the smallest of feathers in the cap I never wear. After they both smoked me at card games since we'd been there, both Amy and Jenn commented on their compassion to give me a chance to let me win once in a while. Even if it was true, I'd have no trouble taking it.

The Hunters Bar also serves food. For such a rustic place, the food was honestly pretty decent. I just got an SOB Burger with tots. It had an awesome worm pit of cooked onions atop the burger and cheese. Really tasty.

Jenn got a burger without the bun. She ordered onion rings she could not eat, per my request, so I had both tots and rings. Even better, I got tartar sauce to dip them. There are times in one's life when ketchup has to take a back seat.

Amy got their nachos, minus the olives. For reasons I've never understood, none of her family likes olives. I like olives very well, not that I have to have my daily fix or something like that. I've been known to go YEARS without an olive, since marrying Amy. Somehow, I've survived just fine in an oliveless world. Go figure!

A couple years earlier, Amy and I shared a Super Nacho plate at a Sequim restaurant. She kept moving the olives, fresh tomatoes and jalapeno slices over to my side of the feast. Them's the best part besides the cheese, meat and chips. And salsa.

Amy got more salsa than served. Yummy! We dined, then finished our game of pool. We'd left our cues on the table alongside the resting balls who knew they would traverse the felt longer than usual with our grades of expertise. Who cares. We had fun, if only to violate any standards of excellence pool tables and other pool players demand. No others waited to play. No others watched us play. We had the whole world in that room to ourselves.

Leaving the Hunters Bar, Jenn continued through town to show us a truly stunning park beside the Columbia River. She said the water was so smooth because a dam had made it into kind of a lake, or bay. It had an official lake-like name the locals use, but you'll never find it on a GPS.

Lovely park. Lots of green grass. Ponderosa pines all over. Flush toilets and watery sinks. Only a couple other people there.

Amy's trying a new craft, making pinecones into painted flowers. She has been collecting pinecones around Sequim which are mostly small to medium sized. The ponderosa pine pinecones were much larger, so she collected a bunch in her dress which were loaded onto a towel which eventually got loaded, towel and all, into a storage hold of Morris.

Crafters who collect their pinecones instead of buying them at Michael's, have to soak them in a vinegar and water solution to get the bugs out. Then, they're baked. I just learned that those open pinecones you see that are open on the ground, close up again when wet. I'm not like a pinecone authority, I'm glad to admit. One who does not try to make pinecones into craft items is required to keep their wits even while the rest of the world focuses on pinecone logic.

I don't even know what that last sentence means.

Full of bar food and drink we headed back to J&J's. J&J have 28 acres for their doggies business. Plenty of undeveloped space that's delightful to hike through. They have a sweet view looking down on the Columbia River from their property. It's still pretty rustic, (there's that word again). The dogs have nicer dwellings than the humans.

Earlier this day, Jenn mentioned Jay and her wanted to commit part of their property to starting a vineyard. They had the exact location in mind – one she pointed out as she drove onto their property. The unfinished, dirt road from the highway to their lodgings drives past the projected vineyard site.

So, on the way back to her home, Jenn took a side trip to show us another vineyard. Sweet green, we could only get close enough to see it from afar. Jay and Jenn have not been successful having a water well dug on their property. They drilled for one and found nothing. Or, they found water and kept drilling, as Jay told me during an earlier visit. Eventually they'll have the water for their home, the doggies, vineyards and any other such ventures.

Right now, they have two large containers strapped to two trailers which they take to a local business with a well who welcomed them to take all the water they liked, not during business hours. So, Jenn and Amy went for another load of water while I worked on this book.

Returning to the J&J stead, we snacked for dinner. The ceiling lights in Morris were getting dimmer and dimmer. Apparently, my house batteries or the AC/DC converter are not doing their job. The batteries we'd bought when visiting J&J in 2021 during our COVID Escape Tour. We drove to Spokane for the day and got 2 new batteries at Costco. I took pics of how it was connected so I'd reattach everything correctly.

It worked just fine, but after the RV was plugged in at home for days before we left, plus the long drive to Fruitland, it should have been plenty of charging time for the batteries. The house batteries on Morris are fairly easy to get to. The power converter I still have not found which is probably why they're not charging. The connecting cables might also be the problem, but I did not bring any electronic tools to check current and continuity. That will have to wait until I get home.

In lieu of buying another battery charger, Jenn loaned us a solar panel for charging the batteries. I did not charge them at their home which was more than drenched with sunlight, so we guessed the now replaced batteries were done for. We'll see when we drive the rest of the trek tomorrow to Glacier.

Without decent ceiling lights, we used flashlights and played a tiles game called Qwirkle. I'd never won a game before, but got good tiles and squeaked out a win tonight for the first time. The flashlights performed admirably.

Earlier, before dark, I checked the water pump. It still worked and neither hose connection showed signs of leaking. Yet, the damp floor kept getting saturated with water. Amy would sop it up with towels again only to have it drenched within the hour.

So, checking the water pump, I unscrewed it from its wooden base to inspect underneath. Lifting it, I saw lots of drops of water escape in the region of the plastic. Clearly I had found the source of water soaking the carpet. The wet wood foundation for the pump probably gave me more of a clue where the water came from than I first realized. I tend to have to think through things for a spell before the reality becomes realized. It took a day before I unscrewed the pump from its foundation and saw the leaking water. C'est la vie. That's just me.

Being we were on vacation, I would have preferred to ignore the problem until we got home. This was not one of those occasions. You know how stinky wet carpet gets, and Amy's nose is more sensitive than mine. She obsessed over soaking up the water far more than moi. We had towels hanging wherever we thought we could hang them without getting other areas of Morris wet.

Nope. This could not wait another week. It had to be fixed tomorrow.

Thursday, July 10, 2025
On the Road to Glacier National Park

For those of you who don't know, getting an RV ready to travel is not a quick job. Not that it's like getting a SpaceX ship ready for launch, but one must check and secure before leaving, both inside and out. I wonder what we would do if the Zombie Apocalypse suddenly appeared and we had to drive to get away quickly. (Keep the diesel and the propane filled, ready to go.)

Yeah. Right.

I made the mistake of leaving my driveway a few years back without taking the walkaround. I started to back out of the driveway and suddenly heard the sound of the electric power cord coming undone. I yanked it out of the RV, still connected to the power outlet on the house.

Dumb! Dumb! Dumb! Dumb! Dumb!

The wires on Morris were not long and it took a bit to get everything reconnected. I also had to secure the power line better, not that it would keep the RV tethered if I again tried to leave still plugged in, but as the anchor for the electric line, my little wire caps repair job would not come off so easily.

Inside, you just want to make sure everything will not roll or move about while you're driving. Depending on how tidy you are, that could take minutes or better part of an hour to stow everything.

Outside, you have to make sure the electric cord is unplugged and stowed. I had the water hose to disconnect. That one takes channel locks to unscrew the connection to the RV. There are exterior doors with stowage compartments that have to be secured. It takes extra time to leave in a motor home.

We also had the cargo carrier on the back. With the generator, two 5-gallon propane tanks and two packages of firewood, I worried a bit about it rocking left and right. I found I'd brought a tie down, so connected the belt to the cargo carrier and the RV ladder, synched tightly to keep it from rocking quite so much. Not perfect, but better. I would have figured out something for a strap on the driver side as well, but there's nothing to connect to as good as the ladder on that side.

The generator and propane tanks really needed to be secured down. When we arrived at J&J's, our one propane tank was on its side. I had it secured top and bottom. It was fine last time we stopped. I always check the load when we stop for gas, food, potty break – whatever. It was doing fine. Morris bounced around the most entering J&J's long, unpaved driveway. We guessed that was when it fell over. Jenn loaned us another 5-gallon propane tank, so I secured both top, bottom and in the middle. They made it to the Montana campground just fine.

Of course, we had tearful hugs and goodbyes. I got to say good-bye to the kenneled dogs. Henry, the one dog who roams freely, made the rounds of love to all three of us. Since Jay could not see us, plans were made to meet up with them on our way home. They live an hour or so north of I-90, so would pick a spot and meet up with us somewhere on our way back. TBD. They would get back the things they loaned to us for the trip and we'd have at least a few precious minutes with my brother. Very nice.

I don't know if you've taken the drive to northwest Montana. From Fruitland, the GPS said to go the northern route rather than head south to I-90. We needed to stop in Spokane, so headed south through Davenport, WA. From Fruitland, it's wooded areas, then the trees disappear and give way to rolling hills. I don't think they were farmlands. Just no trees. We saw a similar area between Cle

Elem and Ellensburg. From west of Seattle to Cle Elum, it's wooded. Then, in the dozen-odd miles to Ellensburg, the trees totally stop and the land is yellow, clear and dry to and Ellensburg and beyond.

Passing through Davenport, I turned right into town instead of left towards Spokane. Amy needed her morning coffee. Near the west side of town, we found a nice coffee place, got juiced up, and headed back east through town.

The trip to Spokane is unremarkable. There's one town in between to slow you down for the mile or two. Most drivers just pass through. Then further along, you start to see businesses crop up like flowering weeds along the roadway. Soon the businesses become a steady border for each side of the highway. There's an air force base on the south side of the highway in western Spokane. Eventually, Highway 2 meets I-90. A few miles further, and we exited for Costco.

Four years earlier, during out COVID Escape Tour, we bought 2 vehicle batteries at that Costco. They checked the record and saw that there was only a one-year warrantee on the batteries. We would have to buy new ones.

I recalled, back in 2021 when we bought those batteries, we bought the most basic pair. You can spend a bunch of money for Lithium batteries. For the most part, they are more reliable and hold a much longer charge and all the other good things we want in a battery, but they have one major flaw (besides the exorbitant price). They fail to work below 40 degrees Fahrenheit. It's not like Amy and I do a bunch of RV camping or traveling during the winter, but that could totally become a problem if the Zombie Apocalypse attacked during such inclement weather.

The other reason we bought the cheaper batteries four years earlier was because our original plan had been to take this memorable trip, then sell the RV. Four years later, we still have him. Going in we knew for this Costco visit, we would still get the basic batteries.

And yes, we know we could have gone to any Costco in the nation. It just worked out that we needed the replacement batteries while we were on this trip and visiting with J&J.

Also, even if the converter is bad, the charge on the new batteries, especially if recharged with the solar panels, will more than get us through this camping vacation.

Our old RV has three vehicle batteries. One is for the engine, and two, called House Batteries, are for the interior lights and such. In many RV's, the batteries can be terribly hard to find and get to and change. Morris, who has his less than admirable designs, (like the brake master cylinder), keeps all three batteries in the very roomy front of the vehicle. Not too difficult to change.

Having 2 House Batteries, they have to be wired/cabled to make a deeper cell 12-volt system. Batteries can also be wired to give 24 volts – too much power that would screw up everything on board. When buying batteries, you pay an extra $15 per battery if you do not exchange your old batteries for the new ones. Thus, I extracted the batteries to take into Costco. I took pictures of the battery connections before removing them. I could easily foresee myself reconnecting things wrong.

Batteries purchased, we put them back in easily enough, tested and got on our way.
While at Costco, I kept an eye out for Donnie or Nancy Sophia Emerson. Not that I really thought I'd run into them, but one never knows.

Amy was famished, so finding something yummy to break our daily fast became next priority. Diesel fuel prices in Washington State were around 70-90 cents a gallon higher than Idaho (or

Montana), so I'd planned to stop around Coeur d'Alene to refuel – maybe 20 minutes down the road. Still, brunch sounded like the best choice before leaving town.

We found a Mexican restaurant to go. Don't those always beat Taco Bell or Taco Time? No contest.

I got a supreme quesadilla so I could eat while driving. Amy got an enchilada platter with an extra taco.

True to form, I stopped to refuel at Maverick barely over the Idaho border. The fuel prices I'd seen in Washington ranged from $4.49 – over 5 bucks a gallon. Maverick displayed $3.69 a gallon – right there with the lowest prices we would see the rest of the day, and more than the 70-90 cents savings I'd expected and just mentioned.

The Visa card was preapproved for $175, so I stopped there. That's around 44 gallons, which translates to around 440 miles. That is more than enough to get us to Glacier and back. I planned to refuel again before leaving Idaho. Top off the tank to get us home.

Traveling in a motorhome has conveniences no other vehicle offers. Specifically, bathrooms. My wife can use the bathroom while we keep moving forward. No special potty stops along the way, and I'd go when we stopped for something.

Before we left, Jenn told Amy about a touristy stop called St. Regis, that advertises the best huckleberry shakes ever. Huckleberries are a BIG crop in this region. Kind of like cranberries in Maine or potatoes in Idaho. Where we live in Sequim, lavender is the biggie. In Whatcom County, where we lived before moving to Sequim, raspberries are a major crop. I learned quite some years back now, that 75% of the raspberries grown in the US come from Washington State, and in state, 85% of the raspberries are grown in Whatcom County.

Some years back, I lived in an RV park right by a raspberry field north of Bellingham, WA. Yum!

In NW Montana, huckleberries are king. I'm not like a big huckleberry fan, but Jenn told us about the best huckleberry shakes in the world, so we stopped, checked out the shops and got our huckleberry shakes. Pretty good.

And, my mind regularly reminded me of Val Kilmer's role as Doc Holiday in Tombstone when he twice recited, "I'm your huckleberry."

On the road again, we would be zooming forth. Amy received text message from the RV park we were racing towards, asking when we thought we would be arriving. We guessed between 7 and 8 p.m. She called and left message.

The ride is striking. So much to see. GPS took us alongside the Flathead Lake – a large lake surrounded by mountains, so amazingly - no real town, but houses upon houses lining both sides of this sizable lake.

Leaving the lake region, it appeared we would get some rain. We did not want the generator to get soaked, so stopped roadside, and covered it with a very old brown tarp I had. I held it on with extra bungees and covered the holes with duct tape. Just as I finished, I walked by the fuel hole. The fuel cap was missing. AGAIN! I don't know what it is about me, but at home with our cars, I **never** forget to replace the gas cap, but in Morris, this is the fourth time I've left the gas cap at the fueling station. It's maddening! And irritating.

I covered the hole with aluminum foil, then literally taped it closed with duct tape until I could get another gas cap. Rain water in the system is never good.

True to its design, the GPS brought us to Mountain Meadows RV Park in Hungry Horse, Montana. We arrived around a quarter to nine. The proprietor, Tom, boarded an electric vehicle and led us directly to Space 20. Pretty level spot, so we did not have to do much leveling of Morris. Old RV's are always a bit of a pain to level.

It's a drive through camp spot, kind of on the corner of three roads, so the space narrows down low where they placed the fire pit. It has electricity, water and a picnic table. I set-up everything, including the solar panel Jenn loaned us, (the new Costco batteries were not fully charged – about half charge. Again, after that long a drive, something is not connecting or working right, but with the solar panels charging the battery every day, it should more than get us through the next five days. We leave the morning of the 6th day – July 16th, and probably won't need the House Batteries heading home. TBD.

Bad News – Amy went back to her side of the bed and felt squishy water in the carpet. She went to sopping it up, going through most of the towels we'd brought, plus a bunch of paper towels.

Later, she checked again and found more water. We had taken showers in the RV and I wondered if that was the culprit. We put fans on it to try to dry it out before it got too stinky.

Amy and Henry in Fruitland, WA

Visiting with Jennifer in Fruitland, WA

Huckleberry Shakes in St. Regis, MT

Friday, July 11, 2025
Mountain Meadows RV Park and Hungry Horse Dam

More water on the carpet in the morning. Amy set to sopping-up even more. The shower theory was not panning out, so I looked under the bed.

In our old motor home, the clean water tank is under the bed. We started to wonder if that was leaking. We'd filled it up before leaving and water was clearly exiting faster than we were using it. But, a hole in the tank seemed very, very unlikely.

Long story short, I discovered the water pump that is mounted in front of the clean water tank was leaking from the plastic side of the pump – from whatever is underneath the plastic skin. That's a problem that cannot be ignored until we got home.

I checked online. Kalispel, Montana is an RV rich environment. There are tons of RV dealers which have parts shops. There are RV parks throughout the area. LOTS of people have RV's there, whether trailers or motor homes or whatever. I cannot imagine living in an RV in that region all winter, but there were plenty who do.

I checked online. Blue Compass RV was the closest, so we headed there and found the pump we needed for 100 bucks. We could have gotten it for say $65 bucks on Amazon, but did not have the luxury of time. Still, one big notable about Montana is no sales tax. We paid exactly 100 bucks for the item.

I was anxious to get back to swap it out, but life is still life. We had brunch at the Nite Owl & Back Room Restaurant and Casino in Columbia Fall. Busy place. Decent food for the price.

One fun feature, a table of 8 or 10 diners sat next to us. A self-driven device came to their table, loaded with their ordered items. The waitress came up, grabbing each dish to serve it. When everything was served, she pressed a button or two on the device and it went back to its home base. Fun! I'd heard of such robotic machines, but had never seen one.

Gas prices in Montana are far cheaper than Washington, but I was amazed how expensive the prices in the grocery store. Typically, when fuel prices are lower, ie, less shipping costs, the market items prices are also reduced. Not in Northwestern Montana. Some of the highest grocery prices I've ever seen.

Amy considered splurging on steaks for her sister's arrival dinner tomorrow. Not at over 20 bucks a pound just for sirloin. We settled on chicken legs. Still 7 bucks a pound.

I won't bore you any further with a trip to the different stores, including Ace Hardware and Autozone (for a gas cap). Leaving town, we decided to get coffee. We saw the Montana Coffee Company. Looked perfect. They even had ample parking in the shade behind the building. Perfect! Then, we found the place closed. It closed daily at 2 p.m.

I had recalled seeing another coffee nook across the street, in the Packmule Liquor & Wine store. Kind of weird, but okay. They had a drive thru. Not usually a good fit for a large motor home, so we walked in. It's like they hid the doorway into the coffee shop behind the shelves of liquor.

Hot day, for us. Living on the Olympic Peninsula, we are a bit spoiled, weatherwise. It seldom gets very hot there. Montana is not blistering by any stretch, but hotter than we're typically accustomed to. A cold coffee drink would help.

The bistro was actually quite warm inside as well. We got a couple cold drinks – Amy preferred iced and I preferred blended. Perfect for the stroll across the street and the drive back to our campsite.

On the way, we (again) saw the road to the Hungry Horse Dam. 4 miles off the highway. We had plenty of time, so drove the 4 mile, slow and winding road up to the dam. Not much traffic up there, so easily found a parking place. Across the dam, there's plenty of parking as well.

The Hungry Horse Dam was built in 1953. It's 564 feet tall. It dams the South Fork of the Flathead River and creates the Hungry Horse Reservoir. There's a small power plant at the bottom, where the river water comes out.

It's a nice stroll across and not too hot. We got there too late to see the exhibits which close like around 4 or 4:30, but were not disappointed to just trek across the dam.

Watery dams are interesting to encounter. On one side, you look down a few feet to the water. You could readily jump in. On the other side, the ultimate skate board run.

It's humorous to see regularly posted signs along one side of the posted dam sidewalk telling us to NOT climb on the parapet wall. "Please keep off the parapet wall." Then, I noticed walking back across, that there are no such signs on the water side.

We got ice at the Canyon Foods Supermarket in Hungry Horse, then returned to the camp so I could replace the water pump.

As mentioned, this was a job that could not be put off. I was so good. So responsible. You would have been thoroughly impressed. I grabbed a white plastic garbage bag and a plush towel and laid them under the pump so the little bit of water that came out when I disconnected the hoses would not add to the already wet and stinky carpet. The old pump was already disconnected from the floor. I just had to unattach the two hoses and hook up the wires.

I'd gotten Teflon tape to make a clean and tight seal on both sides of the new pump. No water was going to escape as soon as I hooked up those two lines. Oh yeah.

I had my channel locks to help me loosen and remove the water lines. The first one came off just fine. Then, I discovered as I removed the second one that I'd not turned off the water. It poured out full strength, like turning on a garden hose.

OH NO!

Dumb! Dumb! Dumb! Dumb! Dumb! Dumb!

I tried to hook it back up. What a vain joke. It's a plastic line, so cannot be kinked like a garden hose. I had to drop it on the already pretty wet towel and run outside to shut off the water feed. A good, long minute of water rushing out of a "garden hose" put a whole bunch more water in there than I wanted or needed. Lots of unsavory emotions racing through the gambits of my brain for sure. A few of those emotions became bad words out of my mouth.

It's not that I did not think about it. For reasons I cannot explain, I honestly thought that the water line bringing water in did not need the pump, so bypassed it. Apparently not.
That's a lesson I will not quickly forget.

Like in NEVER.

I finished replacing the pump and turned the water back on to make sure it did not leak. When done right, it turned out perfectly. We tested it. Amy wondered why she could not hear it. The old pump was not loud, but clearly running. I read that the new pumps were much quieter. Alright by me.
There was some plastic sheeting under the bed, by the old pump, supposedly meant to catch the water in case it leaked. Big sections of the plastic sheeting were missing or torn, so no longer able to prevent further watery changes. This is one of

those, "I'll put down new plastic someday when I have nothing better to do." (Translation: It Ain't Ever Gettin' Done, I 'Spect).

Being our last day before Carrie and family arrived, we made a small fire and cooked sausages and corn on the cob. Plenty yum for the two of us. A little time watching the flames, then headed in for the night.

There were little mosquitoes – not many, but there. If they bit you, it itched for a short time, then seemed fine. We still donned Off! and kept any at bay. After the fire burned down, we stirred it up and enjoyed a quiet evening in, watching some YouTube videos until Amy fell asleep. Then, I got to do a little more typing on this book.

Hungry Horse Dam, Montana

Hungry Horse Post Office

Saturday, July 12, 2025
Carrie, Nate and Emi Arrived

Not to belabor the facts, I'll mention one more time that we still had to dry out the carpet, so after both of us arose, we lifted the bed and set the fans to try to dry out whatever it could.

We had some time before Carrie, Nate and Emi would arrive, so went back into town for ice and such. There was a zipline place along the highway we passed daily. Amy, Carrie and Emi wanted to do the zip line. I'm too heavy, and Amy indicated Nate was not interested.

Right next door to the Zipline place was a touristy rock and crystals shop. Very nicely done, actually. The polished rocks and crystals were amazing. Some very expensive. We just stopped in to check it out and discovered a Vortex Tour they offered. Neither of us had any idea what a Vortex Tour entailed.

The proprietor pointed to a little info paper posted, plus prices. 15 bucks for adults. 10 bucks for kids. Not bad if it was worth anything.

The door at the back of the shop led to the Vortex area. Amy asked a few people who left the tour whether it was worth it. Everyone gave it rave reviews and said it was definitely worth it, so we decided to go through it after Carrie and group arrived.

The rock shop was perfect for finding a gift for Quinnlyn, our daughter back in Sequim. She LOVES such rock work. Amy got a bracelet for herself and a smooth stone for tension and stress, but nothing grabbed her for Quinnlyn, (within the affordable items).

Carrie gave us regular ETA's, so we headed back to camp.

I was sitting by the cold fire pit when a car stopped. A woman in sunglasses exited whom I first thought was Carrie. Nope! It was one of her work friends from the Air Force, named Britney. They'd been stationed together 23 years earlier and had not seen each other since. What a grand reunion!

Carrie and family came a dozen minutes later in Nate's big Ford truck – a very expensive Black Ops package Ford vehicle. He'd gotten it just before we saw them over Thanksgiving in Omaha, in 2023. Very fancy. Total bells and whistles.

Nate's included a Tonneau cover on the back that locked.

I asked the question long time back, whyizit we don't make pickup trucks with locking covers?

Nate's may have been the first one I'd knowingly seen. Being able to lock up the contents in the back of one's pickup truck seems like something that should have been addressed and corrected long before any of us were born.

My 2004 Dodge Ram has a nice cover, but there's no way to lock the tailgate. If I could lock the tailgate, the cover would provide more than adequate protection for anything in the bed.

I had Britney move her car around to the front of Morris. The back had a perfect spot for Nate's big pickup.

I should mention that our camp was not completely secluded from all other camps, but it still felt like it kinda stood apart on its own. We could see other campers across the road, but none were close enough to strike up polite conversations. Many of the campsites were like side-by-side parking places. Our closest neighbors were across the dirt road. No one above us that we could see.

Directly across from our camp was a covered parking space. A large motorhome parked there and we first presumed it was a campsite, but nope. It was just a place to park RV's, which included a high, wooden carport.

One of the days there, a man came and worked on the back of the RV. One day it was gone and the next day, a different RV parked there. Apparently, it became a work space for the RV Park.

That gave plenty of room for Nate to back in his truck.

Thus far, Amy and I had only shared the RV with Emi when she came to visit last year. One little girl is easy to add to the living space, but three made the space much more challenging to do anything. The couch would be Carrie and Nate's bed. It laid down into a small double bed. I also had to figure out how to turn the dining table into a bed. I knew of its design but had not needed it before that day. Fortunately, it was remarkably easy. My hats off to Tiffin Allegro. Sometimes the designs actually make sense.

Before we made the bed for Emi, I told her she would be sleeping on the dash-board. Of course she objected. Actually, it would be more than enough space for her little being. I've heard more than a few stories of friends whose kids or grandkids slept on the dashboard. For many, it was their favorite bed in the RV.

35-year-old Morris has 2 accordion doors - one for the bedroom and one for the bathroom which is positioned directly forward of the bedroom, and aft of the kitchen/living space. They dangle from the ceiling along a runner when they work right. The second one has been off its track for years.

I worked it back on right after we got Morris. It stayed all of x minutes, then hung limply when not tied up to the bulkhead. For Amy and moi, no biggie, but now we all needed some privacy. I messed with it briefly and was reminded why it didn't work. So, everyone just pulled it across and kind of tried to lean it against the doorway by the fridge. That worked about as well as losing weight by learning how to use Photoshop and AI to make yourself look slimmer.

The other accordion door for the bedroom worked perfectly. We had never used it before, and I'm not sure any of our predecessors used it much as well.

What's lame is that after the few days with Carrie and Nate, it then occurred to me how to make the broken door more functional. All it would take is a few Neodymium magnets and some contact cement. Then, it would stand tall and strong when we needed it to and be very easy to disconnect for access.

The strap to hold either door open worked just fine. I added the magnet after we got home. Carrie loves to put as much into her trip as she can. She's a go getter who typically hates to leave any minute unplanned and filled with whatever she wants to do. But this day, after traveling up from Yellowstone, they were very content to hang by the fire and visit with Britney. (I hope I'm spelling her name right. I didn't ask).

First night there, they were content to hang like we were camping. We cooked up the chicken wings and snacked on other edibles that probably are not that good for anyone's body. The fire again was a bit of a challenge to get burning, but it served for the evening.

Amy always posts pics of our adventures on Facebook. She does that during the year, whatever is happening, but more so when we travel. She posted tons during the Amy and Dave COVID Escape Tour – 2021, and during the Amy and Dave Portugal Escape Tour – 2023.

This time she received a comment from one of her coworkers who said she was at Swan Lake – a family property less than an hour south of our campsite. She invited us to join them on the lake, take a boat ride and have taco dinner with them.

Amy discussed it with Carrie and Britney, and all agreed to go tomorrow.

Likewise, we planned to get together for breakfast in the morning. Britney would be there by 8 a.m.

Emi went in to bed on the couch bed before anyone noticed. They moved her to the dining table bed. Nate and Carrie went to bed together, but Carrie eventually joined smaller Emi on the dining table bed. More room, I'm guessing.

Another distinction of Morris is that the heater works really well – in the main part of the motorhome, but in the bedroom, it only blows cold, unheated air. There are two thermostats on board – one above the couch, and the other in the bedroom. Both seem to work, but the bedroom does not blow warm air.

It was summer and not that cold, so the heater was not that big a deal. We had plenty of blankets to keep us warm. Before Carrie and family arrived, we turned on the living room heater and it warmed the entire RV just fine. Now that we were closing up the rooms, the living room heater could not make it back to the bedroom.

Really, the only time we perhaps needed the heater was in the morning. Overnight, the RV got a bit cool. Again, the blankets were well enough to keep us warm, but the heater certainly was appreciated. Sometimes Nate thought it too warm in there. Now, That's an endorsement.

    Amy and I nestled together in bed, closed in by ourselves, watching YouTube on her tablet. Really roughing it.

Sunday, July 13, 2025
Swan Lake, Montana

    8 a.m. came early enough. Britney showed up on time. I don't know where she was lodging. She lives in Helena, MT, the state capital.

    Nate took the reins to make breakfast. They'd brought their Blackstone stove – a flat cook surface perfect for making pancakes. It uses the small propane bottles you can buy at Walmart or wherever. They cooked up some bacon and pancakes.

    Amy is Gluten Free, so we had brought gluten free pancake mix from Trader Joe's. Very yummy. One of the better GF pancake mixes. Nate used that to make the pancakes. Carrie is not as gluten intolerant as Amy, but she feels better when she avoids eating wheat as well. Amy had Crone's Disease years earlier which totally made her gut more sensitive to some foods.

    It also turned out that we'd forgotten to bring maple syrup. I remembered it back home, but somehow it joined that short list of items one forgets. (I also forgot to bring pop can sleeves. Emi asked about one and I realized I'd considered it but did not bring any).

Fortunately, Britney brought some Mrs. Butterworth and Carrie had a homemade mixed berry syrup. Notably, everyone went for the homemade syrup over the buttery Mrs. B's.

Bringing our RV is not that easy to drive around, plus we were still dealing with the flooding in our bedroom which made the small room a bit more musty. Thus, the five of us piled into Carrie and Nate's very fancy pickup. We could leave the fans running on the bedroom carpet.

I love exploring places I've never visited. The drive is always so intriguing. Most of us know how boring and uninspiring it can be driving the same, old trails surrounding our lives. New places are typically inspiring to me.

We headed down to Swan Lake and found the property easily enough. Ain't GPS wonderful. Nate lives with it on his truck display everywhere we goes.

They had a sweet dog named Baron. We also met Erica's dad, Rod, who seemed more than glad to have some new company. We all visited inside for a short spell, then changed clothes and went down to the water. The sun shone brightly, but it was not too hot. Their son, Kellen, and Emi sat atop a large floater to be dragged behind the boat. I decided to stay on shore and watched as they raced around the close-by waters.

The large floater looked a bit less inflated than may have been ideal. That proved to be true as the floater flipped over. Emi and Kellen had their life vests, and both were also decent swimmers. They righted the floater, got aboard again and were slowly brought back to the dock.

They had three large floaters. Changing out for one that was better inflated, Amy and Erica's husband, Drew, joined the two kids to be towed about behind the boat. They had a splash cooled ride for the next half hour.

Returning to shore, we helped get everything stowed away. Amy found a few more pinecones to take home. We headed to the house. I got to sit with daddy Rod, sipping a beer and talking about their family home, his career and more. Tacos are conveniently easy to prepare, and we all feasted in a large back room of the house that has windows all the way down overlooking the lake. They have a huge dining table set up with ample seating for all there and more.

A bit more visiting and another beer, then we were on our way back to camp.

I'm pretty good at starting campfires, but for whatever reason, this wood does not want to burn. I used up all the paper I'd brought, which was not much but should have been more than enough for our trip. I had a Sudoku puzzle book. I only work the hardest puzzles, so the front puzzles became kindling fodder.

Amy got me this wonderful stool for playing guitar. She suggested we bring it along.
I don't know if any of you have ever tried to play a guitar in a camp chair. It's obnoxious. Preferably, I'd rather not have arms on the chair to start. The foldable chairs that sit really low are the worst. Andirondack chairs are terrible for sitting, even if I don't have my guitar. It puzzles me why those chairs are even being sold or who would care to use one?

The stool could have been perfect, but unfortunately the campsite was, well, a campsite with dirt and rocks and tree roots and grassy weeds and whatever. I never found a firm place for the stool, so it mostly sat unoccupied the rest of the vacation.

To my surprise, Emi again crashed out early. The lake day wore her out. Everyone got a cold drink and something to snack on and chatted about their lives and family and whatever while I played guitar strums in the background. Sincerely, that's a pretty nice way to spend an evening.

Monday, July 14, 2025
The Vortex

As you may recall, Saturday Amy and I visited what seemed like a typical tourist trap in Columbia Falls. We told Carrie and family about it, insisting they would love to explore it.

Amy, Carrie and Emi wanted to do the zip line which was right next door to the Vortex store. They checked, but had to make reservations. No times available before everyone left. Perhaps a bit disappointing, but really it was not like the ultimate in zip line scenery. I'm sure it still would have been fun, but they did not miss out on as much as they would have at other zip line sites.

Plus, we had the Vortex to explore. They have tours like every hour or so. Over a dozen attend. It's fifteen bucks per adult and ten for the kids. The money could be very well spent, or a total rip-off. This time, we were more than satisfied.

I've heard about such places before, but never gave them much attention. They sounded a bit suspect, to be honest. A tour guide takes you through to see all the sites, then leaves you to stay as long as you want on your own, which I find most admirable.

I guess I should try to describe what the attraction is. In different parts of the world, there are multiple electromagnetic vortexes, or vortices gather in like a one acre area. The flow in a spiral motion where unique or even weird things occur in these rare zones.

Our guide took us down a hill then left us for a bit. A recorded message box introduced us regarding the vortex zone, how it was revered by the native Americans, and so forth. The zip line riders rode well above us while we hiked along this section. We continued on down, then did a U-turn to be rejoined by our tour guide.

There was a weird looking house. In front of the house was an area 6-8 feet wide marked off. The guide used a long level to show the ground was perfectly level. Then, he said that if someone stood on one side, they would appear shorter versus the other side. They started with a few kids, standing facing each other. One became notably shorter than the other, then they changed sides and equally changed heights. It was fun.

He asked for other volunteers, and I shamelessly stepped forward. The first adult to join in. Nate joined me, facing the other side. Standing on the spot, you can detect it, but seeing the videos and pictures on Amy and Carrie's phones thereafter showed how much our heights seemed to change. With that said, it was still fun to look at Nate more eye to eye, then change sides and seem to tower over him a bit more.

Next, the guide took us into the weird, wooden cabin. It resembles a funhouse, like you might visit at the amusement park. The floor is angled. In the middle of the room is marked the center of that vortex. A person can stand leaning far, far forward, or turn around and look like Neo in The Matrix.

Before the tour, some were given marbles. They could place a marble on a place that seemed to roll uphill. It was interesting, and the vortex likely made a difference, but inside the cabin, it more appeared to me to be just rolling uphill because the cabin was sloped.

There were a few other notables in there. They had a large homemade pendulum. When you pulled it back and let go, it would go twice as far on one side than the other. Even with the angled floor, you could tell the center of the pendulum.

The guide stated that if the pendulum base was weighed on one side, it weighed 3 pounds. On the other side, where it traveled half the distance, it weighed 6 pounds. Now That is something most intriguing.

He also showed us a broom – just an old corn broom, significantly used; the bristles tapered on one side at the bottom. He stood by the pendulum and easily made the broom balance on its bottom all by itself. After his presentation there, he let us explore it a spell before continuing the tour. A mom with kids all took turns standing up the broom on its own.

Finally, there was one small platform along one wall that was actually level. I went and stood on it a bit. All my equilibrium thanked me for the moment.

Moving on with the tour, our next stop was an area 20-25 feet wide. There was a level concrete round paver in the middle, then 6 more pavers surrounding it 10 or so feet away. When someone stood on the center, they could watch others on the perimeter getting noticeably smaller or taller.

That one was a little harder to film because when someone in the circle is standing closer to you, they are automatically larger and taller. I didn't do it, but considered I really should step back another 25 feet, minimum. I totally expect the effect would have been all the more recordable.

On the other hand, still by the circle, they'd placed a vertical flat pole with varying colored tapes, each measuring one inch. The guide explained that the vortex measured two types of people – Wave and Particle. When someone stood by the taped pole, they either became taller or shorter while we all watched.

Cameras were more than welcomed. Amy stood by the pole and we could see her clearly gain an inch or more after 20-30 seconds. Carrie shrunk an inch or so. I grew. To stay the same size became the anomaly in this place. If Wave, they grew. If Particle, they shrunk a bit. But, it was never explained or guessed why some people were Wave and others were Particle.

Next, he took us to a circle of trees, most of which were bent over. He had a small light in his hands. When he touched another person, in this case a boy of around 10, the light lit up. Then, he had everyone on the tour take hands. He joined the circle and the light relit. The power of the vortex flowed through all of us at that stage.

Finally, there was one last circle where many could feel the difference of the vortex when they stood on the perimeter and extended their arms and hands within. Amy could feel it, but I could not.

Then, when I stepped inside the vortex, I put my hands and arms out, and just as quickly, they felt "normal" again. I could clearly feel a change. Kind of fun as well.

After the official tour, we checked out and revisited all the sites over the next hour, then headed out and back to normalcy.

Heading back to camp, we rested a spell, then headed out for dinner in Columbia Falls at the Gunfight Saloon. It sounds like a bar where kids would not be welcome, but the business name has become a carry-over, so families are more than welcome.

To eat, you stand in line and make your orders. There's a large dining room which is where we sat. On the other side, outside tables. A solo guitarist performed on the outside stage. When your order is complete, you pick it up from the serving counter. It's actually an interesting arrangement since it's quite a large establishment. Saves them a bunch of costs on wait staff, I'm sure, but the line to order can get very, very long.

Dinner is always such a nice time to visit together. I had a large beefy sandwich. Some had pizza or a salad. Then, we went next door for ice cream for dessert at Farm to Table Ice Cream as Nate went for the truck. We'd had to park three blocks away there in downtown Columbia Falls.

Returning to the campsite, we lit a fire and sat around in our cozy corner. Emi stayed by the fire with us this evening – for a spell. Carrie and Nate are military officers, so early to bed, early to rise is their standard. I'm a night owl, but glad to hang with them while they were awake.

Here's the layout of our motor home. Our old RV has no pull outs, so it can become a bit tight for 5 people to share. Still far from bad, but less room than Amy and I typically enjoy. Starting at the driver's seat and shotgun, there's a living room area with a convertible couch and a solo, fixed easy chair. The main room becomes the kitchen. Sink and fridge on the driver's side. Dining table with benches for 4 on the shotgun side. As I mentioned earlier, Nate and I figured out how to make the dining table into a bed for the first time. Continuing back is the bathroom, with a toilet, shower and a large closet for hanging clothes, vacuum cleaner and more. Finally, in the back, the one bedroom for Amy and moi. The bed in the middle, your head is meant to lay by the back window. You can stand on each side of the bed. On each side of the bed, there is a clothes cupboard that lights up when you open it, and two drawers. Above the bed is lots of storage room for bedding. The circuit breaker board adorns one side of the bedroom wall. The other side has a small, triangular shelf that had a very small TV when we bought it. I took out the TV and placed an upright fan to oscillate and cool us during our night's slumbers.

For privacy, there are accordion doors between the kitchen and bathroom, and another accordion door between the bedroom and bathroom.

The bedroom is mostly bed, made even more tight when I changed the foam mattress with tapered corners, with a real queen-sized mattress. It fit just fine, but we have to climb over the bed to get in and out of the room.

As I mentioned earlier, I was rather foolish not to see the way to make one of the accordion doors work better while there. The door is well long enough to reach across the doorway and more, but it's kind of flimsy when we tried to stand it up by the fridge. It seemed like it should have been happy to stand there without issue, but it commonly collapsed and made privacy more comical than any of us preferred.

Our bedroom accordion door hung from the ceiling just fine - probably not used much over the years, so we could close it without issue. I was silly to not find a good, or at least better fix while Carrie and Nate were there. After I got home, I took a couple magnets, glued them to the wall by the fridge and the door stuck closed just fine. I'm always amazed how dense I can be sometimes.

C'est la vie.

Note the height difference between the 2 girls on level ground in the Vortex

Tuesday, July 15, 2025
White Water Rafting

Today showed one of the main reasons we took this trip. Both Amy and Carrie really wanted to take a white-water rafting trip. The cost is up there, but not over the top. I just saw a fancy-dancy train trip in Portugal which is €750. They wine and dine you with fancy food and such, but that still seems like a bunch of moolah for a partial day trip on a train. I expect it returns on the same rail, but I digress.

The five of us again loaded into Nate's fancy pickup and headed a dozen miles east to West Glacier.

West Glacier holds one of the main entrance points into Glacier National Park. We were not to head into the park today. That trip is tomorrow. Today, we reached a very busy area in West Glacier where hundreds of people were getting ready for their day on the water.

First, you get outfitted with life jacket and helmet. Later we all got an oar to help paddle. They had five inflatable boats for our tour. Each boat held either 8 or 10 people. We were assigned to an 8-person boat. Each boat has a guide who sits in the aft part of the boat. He or she will first give instructions, then directions to all of us as we go underway.

Everyone checks-in, of course. It's nice for them to know we are there. A little more waiting around. Another visit to the restroom. Grab a quick bite to eat before beginning the adventure.

They load everyone onto buses which head further east along Highway 2, following the Middle Fork of the Flathead River for 14 miles. Most wore their helmets and life jackets. Everyone had an oar sitting beside them. It's a nice, wind-y drive along the riverside. We get to pre-see the tour in reverse for much of the bus ride.

On the bus, one of the tour guides chatted and told jokes to everyone. He seemed like the leader of the pack, but later learned he was one of the underlings. He did not know the river as well as some of the other guides.

Still, he just had a fun wit attached to his outgoing personality, so became the designated Bus Tour Guide. He reminded me of Jolly Jimmy in the Beatles movie, Magical Mystery Tour. Not that he wore any uniform, but he just had that bubbly, comical personality that made the trip more fun.

All of the women he mentioned, including the two female tour guides on the bus, were his "ex-girlfriends." I expect he had A LOT of ex-girlfriends who didn't know they were his girlfriends at the time. Maybe he's living Groundhog Day and this trip was his daily recycled tour. Or not. There were times on the river he was checking with other guides which forked split was the best. If he'd run the river everyday for 20 to 30 years, he would know the best ways to go forward and backwards. The Groundhog Day theory is laid to rest - again.

Approaching destination, they leave the road and drop off everyone by another restroom – the last restroom we will see for the rest of the 8-hour tour. Another truck continues on with the five boats to unload by the water.

Years back, I worked for the courts, both in Utah and Washington State. Part of that employment, I was a court clerk, so sat in court assisting the judge, sometimes for hours. I made a regular practice of visiting the restroom whether I needed to go or not. I am totally sure it was a regular blessing to my days in the courtroom.

Just as a fun and totally unrelated sidenote, the judges in Bellingham, WA were given instruction to take a break after 2 hours or so of court hearings.

Court is not like the TV or movies make it out to be. Just watch a hearing or two on YouTube. Even that will not give you the full picture.

Most court hearings are NOT trials. Criminal trials. Civil trials. Those are the exceptions. Most court hearings are called a stacked calendar where multiple cases are heard. They might be criminal arraignments, pre-trial hearings, or guilty pleas, one after another. You'll see like 40 or 50 cases processed in a morning hearing. That means you have a courtroom full of people.

The judges were instructed to give the clerks a potty break after 2 or so hours. Then, they left the Bench and went back into Chambers. Chambers is a fancy, antiquated word for their office. What apparently missed their attention was that the clerk is responsible for the 40-50 file folders they brought to court and were handing to the judge, processing the court decisions, entering into the computer as well as writing on court documents the minutes of the hearings. Just because the judge left the courtroom does not mean the clerk can just abandon their desk and leave all those files sitting there.

I guess they could bring the files with them, but by this time there are files that have been processed, files partially done and files still awaiting to call the case. I'm not saying it was impossible, but taking those files from the courtroom lent itself to mistakes. Mistakes are a big no-no in the court, as you can imagine.

So, I told the judges after court sessions different days that they take this little break because Labor and Industry says they have to give us a break, but we cannot leave the files in the courtroom unattended. We would have to take the files with us, or empty-out and lock up the courtroom. The judges wisely changed their procedures and we all got out of court a bit faster. Okay! Now that I have that off my chest, back to white water rafting.

Those who needed (or didn't need to) visited the restroom. What was funny is that they just let us out along a dirt road. They dropped us off, but did not give any instructions what to do, whether they would come back with the bus, or ???? Lots of people milling around wondering what was next.

Eventually, we got the call and walked down to the water. The sun was bright, a few clouds and it would be a warm day.

There were three men and two women guides. We got one of them on our boat.

When everyone gets to the water, rafts are assigned. I was pleased to get one of the 8 person rafts (instead of a 10) for reasons that don't matter to anyone else on Earth, (including myself). We were put into our raft while still on the shore for instructions. Our guide, (I think her name was Katie, but my brain may be wrong. Maybe Haley? You'd think I'd remember. Both women guides had the same first name.) Katie, (or Haley) helped arrange our seating. Amy wanted to be one of the front row rowers. I sat along third row right. Nate to the left. Carrie behind us and Emi sitting between Nate and moi. One other family with teen son shared our raft, sitting front and second rows. Of course, the water flowed easily as we pushed on into the real water.

One item I feel important and thankful to mention here: in Amy & Dave's Portugal Escape Tour – 2023, we took a kayak trip in the Algarve to Benagil Cave. It turned out to be a terrible trip for Amy, but I was blessed to ride with our tour guide, Phillipe, because my lower back was so messed up. He did 98% of the rowing.

Now two years later, I'm sitting on a river raft in western Montana with an oar in my hand that

I can actually use without a bunch of pain. Thank You, Jesus, for Your healings!

All 5 rafts milled about in quiet waters, learning the commands to row or not row, etc., until all were ready, then we moseyed down the river.

Not to give away much, there are two sections of this trip. The first part the water is mostly tame and in some places, gets rather shallow. The bottom of the raft found the rocky bottom of the river often. We would have become stuck on the rocks, but Katie showed us a practice they called *Popcorn*. Basically, when we would feel ourselves getting stuck on the thousands of small, smooth river rocks, we all started bouncing, not really in sync. If Popcorn didn't work, the tour guide would drop off the back of raft to push it over the rocks. For us, Popcorn method worked each time. Other rafts got stuck at times and had to be pushed. The end result, we became the lead raft for much of the run.

As I said, I thought the bus tour guide was one of the main, long-time guides, but as we met splits or forks in the river, they would yell to our Katie which way to go. She would point left or right.

Funnily, some still tried going the other way and pretty much every time got stuck on the rocks.

Rafting during this part of the summer, the water had started to taper. Not the spring rush anymore. There would come a time when the water would be so scarce in places I'm not sure they could continue to do the rafting tours, at least in the first section.

We took the full day trip. In hindsight, the half day trip probably would have been fine because there was very little to no white water during the first half. The real rapids all came in the second half of the trip. At one point well through the tour, we saw 5 more of their distinctly colored raft teams come from a side tributary to enter the river a ways ahead of us. They would not have much of the shallow water and a more adventuresome run for sure.

On the other hand, the full day on the water was still pleasant for an older guy like *moi*. Not that the cold splashes we all eventually met were that bad, but it became more of a sightseeing tour of the beautiful southern edge of Glacier National Park.

When Katie told us to row, we seldom rowed more than 5 or 6 strokes. Not much rowing at all. Certainly nothing to wear out anyone's arms. Most rowing had 2 functions: to help straighten our course or avoid the riverside, or to speed us up a bit before hitting a stretch too shallow to row.

I live in a beautiful place of the Earth on the Olympic Peninsula. Lots of trees, rivers, rain forests, ocean access, etc. Hiking galore. Bicycle tours. Nice drives through the mountains or shorelines. Far from any big cities. Seattle is around 2 hours away if we drive through Tacoma over the Tacoma Narrows Bridges.

In turn, for us flowing past endless forest probably was less awesome than the others who lived in less scenic areas. Carrie and family live near Omaha. For them, this could have been a feast for the eyes, (except for Emi – the 9-year-old got bored with all of it after the first hour or so).

As I said, the first half held few exciting moments of river rafting. Roughly halfway through, they set to shore. A large, small rocks area where they would feed us lunch. They brought all the makings and sent all of us out to find wood for the fire. They unfolded these racks that became grills to cook the elk burgers. They had tables I never saw on any of the rafts, with potato salad, chips and other such picnic feastings.

Many went to the wooded areas, first to pee, then to collect wood. I collected a bigger bundle than any other I saw.

The tour guides all worked in sync, making a fire suitable to cook meat and such, as well as set-up the rest of the repast.

The water provided a somewhat calm pool where we landed. Different other tours passed by. Everyone waved and showed they were having a delightful day on the river. I noticed some of our rafters entered the icy waters up to their waist, probably to potty. More women than men entered that water.

I wasn't all that hungry, but still enjoyed the lunch greatly. Many, including myself, sat on the edge of our rafts. I'm unhappy to admit I don't get up off the ground nearly as easily as I used to.
This was also a great place to take pics of everyone. When on the river, yes, we had our phones, but I neglected to mention, Carrie was most prepared, bringing waterproof bags for our phones that rolled up tightly at the top. It kept the phones dry, but it also became less convenient to take pics while on the water.

After everyone had their fill, the tour guides wolfed down a few bites, then cleaned up the lunch site just as quickly as they set it up. The fire doused, we returned to the water.

This would soon take us to the actual whitewater section of the tour. With that said, we were still a couple miles off, so everyone had time for their meals to settle.

There's a part of me that has always wanted to take a whitewater rafting trip. We've all seen the pics of people literally holding onto the sides of the raft for their lives as the huge currents dwarfed the inflatables. They were tossed and spun at the whims of the river.

This tour was not like that. Each set of rapids had a name. I could not recall any of the names, I felt sorry to say, and I could not take notes while I was on the river. Katie said at one point that if an area of the river had a name, it would be rapid. Then, writing this book, I remembered that I bought a T-shirt with the names of the rapids on the back. Tunnel. Bonecrusher. The Big Squeeze. Jaws. Pinball. Repeater. It's also not like I could not have looked them up online, but that felt like cheating for no really valid reason I can conjure.

Most of the rapids stood alone. A couple rapids offered a very brief lull, then back into the moving water.

When we were in the rapids, Katie always told us to row. Again, these were not the most vicious rapids in the world. All of us were sitting on the inflated side of the raft where we could row, no matter how turbulent the water. A few times, I went to row hard, but the water suddenly wasn't there, dipped by the rocks beneath me. I tried to row against nothing but air. I lost balance each time. Fortunately, nothing close to falling in which I would not have relished.

Lots of water splashed up over us. I am amused to think that we paid a bunch of money to have the icy river water wash over us at regular intervals.

As I mentioned, Emi became bored with the river run. Mostly, she sat on the bottom of the boat between her dad and *moi*. During one lull in the tour, Katie asked where everyone was from and what did we most want to see while we were here.

All the adults said the national park or this day on the river. Emi said to see her Aunt Amy and Uncle Dave.

As she sat in the bottom of the boat, she would often nap. I cannot say I felt much compassion for her when the rapids sent some small waves over the side, soaking all of us. Poor Emi was awakened by one of those waves. I'm sure it was a jarring feeling, but I also not so secretly felt a small amount of amusement to see my niece rudely awakened by the stinging cold water.

Amy and the other rower up front on her right got the most of the splashing water. There's a great pic of Amy right after she got splashed by one wave, crying out just in time to get a mouthful of water from the next wave. She would call out when doused, one time her voice gurgled by the next wave flooding her mouth.

Lots of waves of water would rush over the bow as they crashed down into a watery, moving valley.

At one point, the water, moving along, but not the full rapids, Katie yelled and pointed out the photographer standing on the bank taking pics of all of us, available for sale when we got back. Digital photography is such a sweet blessing and far better quality than those pics they used to peddle in amusement parks when you were on the roller coaster or getting doused by a waterfall. Those first amusement park pics clearly looked like you, but they were about as clear as a modern-day surveillance camera, at best.

We also passed some abandoned train tunnels I think would have been fun to explore. Each was marked with large, readable letters on the side of the concrete. I wondered who would have been reading those words? Someone on the water? It was not like there were any roads or trails on our side of the tunnels.

Also, late in the river run, we reached some deeper areas, easily floating forward when a couple guys on the neighboring raft suddenly jumped into the cold water. They easily remained afloat with their life jackets, and soon climbed back onto the raft. None of us were sure, but we were probably still a mile or 2 from the end of the run. The rapids would already have soaked them, so a wet ride the rest of the way hardly mattered. On the other hand, it did not occur to me until later that they both probably just had to pee.

I wish I'd taken pics. If I go again, I'm getting an old GoPro that can handle the water. If we're going to get soaked repeatedly, I want a Bonafide video record.

My only real disappointment with the tour was that we never saw any wildlife. I kept looking for it - even a couple of deer or otters or something, though a bear or cougar would have been best. The only wildlife we saw included lots of birds. Edward Abbey would have been even more disappointed.

Amy surprised me. We'd taken the 14 mile ride upriver. She expected we would be taken back to the base via bus as well. I said, Nope. I expected we would get out of the water and walk from there back into West Glacier. I was correct. It was funny, though. It's not like they really gave us any directions. There were a good-sized group of young people jumping into the water near the overpass which led into the entrance of the park. We turned to shore across from them, still donning our life jackets and helmets and oars and bagged cell phones, to walk up an incline to the road, then had to figure out which way to go. It was not real hard, but we guessed/deduced correctly and made the quarter mile walk or so to the home base.

We washed off our gear before returning. The old bathrooms were a popular stop, but the little, tourist-trappy store was clean and modern. Both Amy and I picked out a T-shirt. As I earlier stated, I got one with the names of the rapids. It only names 6 of the rapids. I'm sure there were more than only 6. Maybe those were the 6 most notable, or the 6 with the more vivid names. Personally, I really like Pinball because it bounced you around back and forth. Bonecrusher was supposed to be the most violent of the bunch - hence the name.

Heading out, dinner time approached. We selected another restaurant in West Glacier, by Highway 2. Nothing fancy, but perfect after our day on the water.

Remarkably, we could see the cars and trucks and RV's and such all lining up a mile back to left turn onto Going to the Sun Road - the entrance to Glacier National Park. The cars coming from the east just seemed to turn when they wanted and did not build the long line-up along the highway.

The long line reminded us what we already knew - to get to Glacier early, before they limited vehicles entering. Not that we would not have gotten in with a little patience, but an early morning rising still suited us just fine.

Back in camp, we relaxed a short time around the fire, but after the long day on the water plus the early rising the next morning, everyone was glad to retire early.

We had planned to play our new cribbage game, but darkness approached. The dining table inside was still a bed which attracted Nate with magnetic strength. I built the fire again. The fire pit was getting a bit more used to us. We got to visit for a bit, but after a day on the water and bellies full, we were glad to retire inside earlier than the other nights.

Except for one BIG mishap.

Nate and Carrie needed some laundry done. Nate took the lead at some point. Mountain Meadows actually has a very nice laundry room. 6 or 7 stacking washers and dryers. I had soap and fabric softener sheets in Morris. They did a load or two of laundry. I saw Nate coming back with his dried laundry and thought, "I need to get some done, too." So, carried down three loads.

When I went back to move the laundry to a dryer, the door was locked. I'd not noticed the sign posted by the door that said it closed up at 9 p.m.

Now this could have been a minor inconvenience, but as I said, our plans for tomorrow were to rise early - well before the laundry room opened, and head to Glacier National Park. We would be long gone before it opened. I was irritated with myself, but had to just take it in stride and call Mountain Meadows in the morning.

I would continue the story in the next day's chapter, but it's just washing clothes. Not a major development in anyone's world.

The next morning while we were in Glacier National Park, I called them and reported my mistake. They were really sweet. It surprised me how nice they were. I told them which washers I'd used. He would transfer the clothes to the dryers and remove and fold them when they were done. Who does that anymore? I'm serious.

After we got back from Glacier, I went and retrieved our clothing. It cost 2 bucks a load to dry them. I offered to pay for it, and they insisted it was not a big deal. The towels were folded and on the counter. The clothing was not folded, but laid out beside the towels. Wow!

I took it back to Morris and laid it on our bed. Later, Amy called me in. A bunch of her clothing was missing. We quickly wondered if the other campers thought it must have been freebies to pick through, not unlike my tenants when I managed rental apartments. I contacted the proprietors and to our relief, discovered he had indeed moved the third washer load to the dryer, but then did not pull it out after it was done. Our third load still hung out in the dryer and I was able to get what was mostly Amy clothes.

Then, as she was folding and putting her clothing away, she found four garments which were not ours. She checked with Carrie. Nope. Not hers either. So, I took them back to the laundry room which was locked up for the night by this time, and left the shirts and women's underwear on the chair by the door. Likely clothing that someone else left in the dryer, hanging out there when my clothes were loaded and dried.

Just as another quick plug for Mountain Meadows, they had their small camp store with both firewood and ice. Somehow, I had failed to see these which were clearly marked outside the store. We had spent lots of time getting both in town. Their prices were less than or equal to lots of places in town. Go figure! When every moment of your vacation is precious, the time saved getting these consumables would have been most appreciated.

I have to also mention, their restroom and showers are better than any other camping site I've ever visited. The showers are included with your stay. They have 2 showers in each main restroom, attached to the check-in, store and the proprietor's home. There's also another smaller restroom which we only used once, not far from the main building. It's closer to the RV dump, but also a nice, little building and facility with a shower on each side.

Good night. We had an early morning drive to finally see Glacier National Park.

WHITE WATER RAFTING

Lunch Time by the
Middle Fork of the Flathead River

Wednesday, July 16, 2025
Glacier National Park – Finally!

Around midnight, we were all awakened by the sound of rain on the RV roof. Lotsa wind. A real storm which was not forecast. Rain had been a suggested, possible maybe in the morning up until that moment. Every time I awoke the rest of the night, I could hear the rain still doing its rapid tap dance above us. I closed the roof vents in the bedroom and bathroom. I also again appreciated that we had old Morris, rather than tent camping.

Rising early, I stepped into the main part of the RV. Nate and Carrie had certainly heard the rain throughout the night, but it never occurred to them the ceiling vent was open. I stepped onto a wet spot of carpet in the kitchen. No biggie. Just cool and wet on bare feet. I shut the ceiling vent while the rain continued to try to splash in.

During the busy summer season, Glacier National Park actually limits the number of cars and trucks that can enter the park. I'd never heard of this before, but apparently the Park Service does not want to overrun the small national park with visitors at any one time.

They start limiting the vehicles at like 7 a.m.

To be more clear, you can enter the park, but there's a point well in the park where the traffic is limited. If you're turned back or don't wait your turn, you just go back the way you came.

So, we intentionally arose early – around 6 a.m., to get into the park before they started limiting visitors. Nobody really knew how far in we would go. We just knew we had to get in before the line started wherever.

More interesting, that's the West Glacier entrance. If you entered by way of the East Glacier entrance, there are no limits. Technically, you could drive around the perimeter of the national park, through some pretty nice countryside, and get in without any hold up. It likely would take longer than just standing in line waiting for your turn to enter, (and that's just a guess), but the east entrance (which has no town specifically attached like the west entrance), has far less visitors. Honestly, I expect most of the people entering from the east side are people who already drove through the entire park from the west side.

I was amazed to learn that there's really only one main road through Glacier National Park – Going to the Sun Road. There are a couple short side roads, like to the Lodge, but for the most part, the whole northern part of the park, all the way to the Canadian border, has no paved roads. No motor vehicles allowed that aren't attached to the park. Hiking access only, and that's a HUGE chunk of real estate to not be able to see except on foot.

There is a road that heads up the west side a ways, and a small section of Highway 17 that clips the northeastern corner, continuing on into Alberta, Canada. We did not explore either of those.

Honestly, I, who love to read maps, totally ignored our Glacier tour possibilities before we drove in. Typically, I would have gaged how we could have seen as much as possible. Not being the driver, I left that to Nate and Carrie. So, we drove where I expect 90% of the tourists drove – in the West Glacier gate, and out the East Gate, then turned around and went back through the way we came.

Fortunately, our tour was not quite that simple, or boring...

First, Carrie is pretty sharp, but (like all of us), sometimes does some very silly things. It's 6 a.m. She wants her morning coffee. We have to get into the park before the 7 a.m. entrance limitations. We have a Keurig coffee maker that makes each cup in less than a minute. She could have made more than enough coffee for the trip before we left camp, but instead she insisted on stopping for coffee. I can appreciate that an official coffee stop should have provided better quality coffee than our homemade coffee, but homemade coffee is better than no coffee.

And, that's what we got.

No coffee.

Except for Amy, who knew better.

No coffee nooks were open, yet. She kept checking en route to West Glacier, and even after we entered the park. Nope. Nobody open to provide brewed bliss. Just to jump ahead a bit, we didn't get coffee until we stopped for breakfast outside the east entrance.

C'est la vie. I like my coffee, but am not one of those who cannot face the day with reasonable emotions without it.

I have a Senior Pass to all US National Parks. It costs 80 bucks. It's good for the rest of my life (unless the country falls into total anarchy, hostile takeover, alien invasion, zombie apocalypse etc., (or I lose it)). It's supposed to be good for up to 4 adults in the vehicle, which included all of us. Children not counted, so Emi was fine. Still, Nate had a pass, too, for himself and Carrie. I don't know if it would have covered Amy and moi. Probably.

Still, I provided my Senior Pass and had to show ID to clarify ownership or age or something.

The rain continued to pour as we drove. Lots of sweet, gray clouds covered the landscape. Sometimes we literally could not see the mountains ahead or beside us because of the clouds.

We saw lots of waterfalls, but I wondered if the smaller ones were only because it was raining. Actually, I should correct that statement. We saw actual waterfalls, but most of the descending water were like vertical streams, flowing rapidly down the mountainside.

Going to the Sun Road follows the southern bank of McDonald Lake for lots of miles. Much of it is still hidden by the trees, but it is a striking and beautiful lake to traverse beside.

The Lodge was still closed when we passed. Sorry Carrie. No Coffee. We continued on.

The road peaks in elevation at Logan Pass. There's a nice parking lot at the top. Restrooms and Visitor Center. Some view areas. For us, though, it was 39 degrees with whipping wind taking the wind chill down quite a bit. We still weathered our way through the wind to the restrooms. Who could say when we'd find another one.

I was totally embarrassed. Sitting shotgun, I opened the door to exit. The wind grabbed hold of my door and slammed it against a very nice looking Subaru. It made a small gouge in their car. Nate's fancy truck seemed untouched.

The owner opened a window and a female hand felt for the gash. Nate spoke with the owners who were amazingly casual about it. Maybe they were driving a rental. Even now, I am touched by that feeling of embarrassment for losing control of the door. I made doubly and triply sure I never lost it again the rest of the day.

We continued on through the park, passing lovely lakes and countless trees. The mountains took back seat as we passed by St. Mary Lake and approached the east entrance, which is also the east exit. We headed out, and drove north a few miles to the town of Babb.

What a fun name!

I wish I'd been at the city council meeting a hundred plus years back when they decided on that name. It is named after Cyrus Babb, an engineer responsible for the St. Mary Irrigation Canal Project. Part of the Bureau of Water Reclamation. Though never incorporated, they got their first post office in 1905.

They had one little café, the Glacier's Edge Café. It's common and nothing fancy. Regular food. Exactly what one would expect for such a small town. It was fairly busy, but had a decent table for all five of us to sit in the rear dining area. Carrie (and Amy) finally got their coffee. Lots of eggs and bacon and such ordered. It's not like we were cold, other than at the Logan Pass stop, but it was still a nice break from the rainy ride.

The two sisters always carry on most of the conversations. Nate's a great guy, but a little aloof to get close to. He's quiet, but not shy. With his position as a Lieutenant Colonel in the US Air Force, he works with Generals and such, so doesn't talk about work. Perhaps the most open times we've shared over the years were during games of cribbage.

Emi got her usual oatmeal. I like oatmeal just fine, but can never see paying for it at any café. No big reason why not. I simply opt for the other hot items.

I do not usually eat breakfast, but by this time of the day, I'm more than ready to eat. Hunger is the best gravy, as cited by Sancho Panza in Man of La Mancha. It really was perfect for the day.

Done with our Babb feast, we headed back into the park. Like I said, I have a Senior Pass that is enough for all of us to enter, but they still checked Nate's pass again as well. Fine by me.

I'm not sure I'll ever quite understand how the drive back through some area seems to go much quicker than the first time exploring. It just does. We stopped again at Logan Pass. The rain had subsided a bit. The wind still blew, yet the temperatures felt a bit warmer as well, so not quite so slicing to visit the restrooms.

No doors damaged this stop.

Carrie, Amy and Emi checked the viewpoint for about 10 seconds. The winds increase to like double in strength from there.

We shared two other notables in our drive back through. First, we stopped at one point that had a mile and a half stroll through the woods. Covered with plenty of cedar trees, it very much reminded me of Washington State. Amy and Emi stayed in the truck.

Carrie, Nate and I enjoyed the stroll and getting out of the truck. No rain. The wet ground fine to hike upon. Then as we passed the restroom, my hand touched my hip pocket, and I realized my wallet was not there.

Isn't that like one of the worst feelings? I don't mean to compare it to losing a loved one – something like that, but in our day-to-day existence, it's a nasty fear.

I realized I'd left my wallet on the seat a bit underneath my leg after we used passes to reenter the national park. That provided only mild comfort. I knew where I'd lost it, but did not know if it had fallen out of the truck when I got out. I started walking all the faster back to the truck. If it had fallen out of the truck, it might still be on the parking place. Foot traffic would be slight enough that no one might have noticed it.
I couldn't get to the truck fast enough.

Actually, I walked right by it. I saw another similarly colored truck that poked its nose out a bit farther, so headed towards that one. Amy saw me pass and called to me.

I got to the truck. No wallet on the pavement. Was this good or bad? I opened the truck door and there sat my wallet, on the floor beside the seat.

WHEW!

That's a biggie, of course, but even more so, I was scheduled to leave town the day after we got back. Flying to Arkansas for a driving job, I would have needed my driver's license. They had to add me as a driver of a Penske in Bentonville before I left town for Grants Pass, OR. If I'd lost my wallet, that would have been a BIG problem for the trip.

Add to that, that the day after I returned from Oregon, I had to leave for Boulder, CO in a UHaul. My friend, John, helps people move out of state. His family situation required he stay home, so asked me to drive the trucks.

DOUBLE WHEW!!

Leaving the hike, we stopped at the Lodge. Nate dropped off the girls and we found a parking spot a couple blocks away.

It's a nice establishment. Big, old wood structures and beams and posts and wall boards provide the rustic but affluent ambience. We dined again just 'cuz we were there. I don't think any of us were all that hungry.

After lunch, the girls toured the usual tourist traps. Nate and I hung out until time to leave.

One key attraction are the red shuttle buses throughout the park. They are most quaint. I'm including a pic, even if it is black and white. Much fun to see.

Also, I am a mosquito magnet. A net in reverse. The mosquitoes think I'm the best meal since sliced bread. No idea why. I am blessed to live in a place with virtually no mosquitoes – a fact I do not know why given all the water about Coastal Washington.

But, on the way back to the truck, I smashed one, oozing red with my blood across my fingers. Nobody else noticed any mosquitoes at all.

You likely never read Amy & Dave's Portugal Escape Tour – 2023. I was viciously attacked there after dark, in Tavira and Faro, down south in the Algarve, by unseen creatures that made my entire skin itchy. If we move to Portugal someday, we will not be able to live in any itchy zone. Further west, from Albufeira on, I had no itchy problems at night. Same anywhere up north, from Lisbon to Sintra to Porto to Coimbra to Nazare'. No attracting flying insects like a bug zapper.

Weird!

It's a divine blessing I would not mind not having quite so abundantly.

As the day progressed, the weather improved. We arrived back at the campsite. I was able to get my laundry that had been locked up the night before.

They were SOOOOO Sweet. He transferred all three loads to the dryers which are placed above the washers. It's 2 bucks per load. They would not take payment. He even pulled out the laundry, folding up the towels and laying the clothing out.

Like I earlier reported, I took it back to Morris, and Amy later realized that a bunch of her clothing was missing. I first presumed that other campers had pawed through it, taking it as freebies. I was wrong. The third dryer load had been untouched and those clothing items sat waiting in the dryer. I got it and brought it back. Most of it was Amy's clothes, so she would have been pretty inconvenienced to have limited garb to wear.

After we got back, everyone was a bit tired, especially after our early rising. Amy, Carrie and Nate took naps. Emi and I went to the campsite store after I got the laundry.

After they declined payment for the dryer loads, we strolled around, looking at the many items on the shelves. Nothing any of us would ever buy, of course.

I suggested getting ice cream. I grabbed a Nestle' ice cream cone. Emi said that was not good ice cream - "good" as in healthy. So, I pulled out a Kirkland ice cream bar. That was acceptable. I said, "Good, (since I had a bunch of those in my freezer back home)."

One of the patrons, an elderly woman watching us, showed great amusement with Emi's stances on acceptable ice cream.

We paid and went across the parking lot to a small pond. Strolling around the pond, we saw lots of little fish. Bigger fish splashed the surface of the water regularly. I'd seen others fishing there during our 5 days stay.

Heading back to the now rested adults, we cleaned up, we headed back towards West Glacier one more time to **Last Best Pizza.**

It's a rustic looking place, just west of West Glacier along Highway 2. It has lots of parking. It's basically a large log cabin – maybe just the façade, but that's good enough for me. Seating outside. Schtuff for kids to do outside, like corn roll game. Nate, Emi and I played a few rounds after we ate.

The menu is a huge blackboard. Most of us ordered pizza or wings and some beer or something to wash it down. They advertised that they had gluten free options for Amy. Unfortunately, they kinda lied. No gluten free pizza, but they did offer gluten free noodles, so she got a pasta dish she could eat. Maybe not what she immediately wanted, but it was tasty and better than some places which can claim they offer gluten free options and when you get there, their only GF menu item is a salad. A green salad is not a meal, no matter however much dressing you smather over it. (Yes, "smather" is not a typo).

It was a bit pricier than the online reviewers told us. I saw only one $ sign, but I would have given it at a second $$.

The food is as good as most anything in the area except maybe the Lodge in Glacier National Park. The seating is just as rustic. The chairs look kind of bulky and took a moment to get your butt settled into, but they were fine. We enjoyed our feast at a large table shared with a family from Southern California. This area would be feast for their eyes versus the hot, dry deserts around their home.

Actually, I really like the desert. It has a delightful charm all its own, not that I want to cross it without sufficient water or something. I'm not planning a holiday in some Sahara Oasis this winter. (Actually, that sounds like of fun now that I think about it).

Part of the fun, of course, are these moments when you chat with people you've never met before and will surely never see again, but for that chance, divine encounter, you get to share a few precious moments of life, eating and drinking and restoring. It's usually some of the best moments of any vacation we enjoy and engage.

During our COVID EscapeTour in 2021, Amy and I had TONS of spontaneous chats with people we passed and encountered. You would have thought we'd all known each other for years.

The family came before us and left before us. Emi should have been hungry enough to eat a horse, but she became picky about the food and had to be coaxed to finish her mac and cheese. She had tons of pizza to pick from as well, plus wings which I love with bleu cheese dressing. (Amy hates bleu cheese and cannot understand how anyone could destroy the perfect flavor of coated chicken wings with such a nasty flavor. For me, it's not wings without my bleu cheese. Ranch is good, but it doesn't cut the palate quite the same).

As you probably know, when you're camping it is not like we have lot of space for storing leftovers. Even in Morris, our fridge can hold a bit, but nothing like a pizza box. As practiced and common travelers, we are always thinking in terms of what we can consume in the moment. It probably reflects how spoiled we are in this nation, and for that matter, most of the western world where we can find food in abundance. We're not rich, but we're not poor, either. We could readily afford to have a pizza and wings feast after a full day on the river raft. I never fail to thank Jesus for His blessings for such days.

Last Best Pizza also had the tourist trap store that we were most happy to peruse. It was not as filled as many stores. They were short on some of the shirts that we probably would have bought. Amy likes purples, violets, lavender, etc. If she finds a shirt in one of those attractive colors that she thinks would be nice, she loves to get it. For her, they were out of the one medium size shirt she liked.

On the other hand, we had not yet bought any gifts for Quinnlyn, our daughter. As I mentioned earlier, this is Huckleberry Country. We saw some huckleberry flavored local honey, so bought two jars, one for us and one for Quinnlyn.

Amy and I also play a lot of cribbage. They had a large cribbage board made out of a barrel slat that was kind of cool, but they wanted $125 for it. Nope. Not in our budget. Then, she spied another one, shaped like a bear head with a bear head sticker and the cribbage holes drilled around the perimeter. Three tracks. Pegs and cards stored underneath. $50. I would not have gotten it, but Amy really liked it. Even better, it had a hanging hole in the back to store it on your wall if wanted.

It's actually a nice game piece to have, but after you buy something, you see the problems that are hidden in the store. First, the bear head sticker is kind of cheap and wants to let go of the wood. We continually press down the borders. It's not fraying or anything, yet. Just not as sticky as it should be.

Second, and this is actually the biggie, we pulled out the playing cards and discovered it had already been sold and returned. The cards were out of order – not a new deck. Worse, the cards were cheap crap. Maybe partially why the game was returned. Or not. Lots of times, people get something just for their holiday, then return it before they leave. It's like people who return their suitcases to Walmart at summer's end, except in the Walmart case, the suitcases really are poorly made and should not have been bought to begin with. If you want a cheap suitcase that is possibly still well made, check out the thrift stores. They typically have lots of travel bags in all sizes. Just a suggestion.

You can also get cheaper suitcases at Ross Dress for Less. Quite the large selection though many are just as cheap quality as Walmart. I'm sure you've noticed, quality Workmanship is not the best way to go for much of life anymore.

Still, for better and worse and in between, we've enjoyed our bear cribbage board. Changing to a better deck of cards certainly was easy and the game is still lots of fun to play.

Some years back, I taught Amy to play cribbage. I learned while in the Navy. We liked the game bunches, as long as one of us doesn't unexplainably have a run of a dozen wins or more. It happens at times with no explainable reason, and is no fun for the loser.

Then, Amy taught Carrie and Nate to play cribbage a few years back. It became one of their favorite card games. When we visited them in Omaha for Thanksgiving in 2023, we had cribbage marathons. They'd learned to play with three players, but never knew they could play teams with four players. That was the most common way to play in the Navy. All four of us could join in; a really nice evening or unsleepy afternoon competition. (I like it better when I win. I'm funny that way).

As the women continued touring the little store, Nate and I took Emi out to play a few games of corn roll toss. I totally beat them all; toasted them thoroughly, (maybe/maybe not, but it's my book, so I can tell the story however I want). =^D

The last night of our Glacier adventure closed with a satisfying aura.

Amy and Emi in the Lodge in Glacier National Park

Group Shot

Carrie and Nate on the 2-mile hike in Glacier

Thursday, July 17, 2025
Heading Home

Last mornings are always times to get everything tidy and packed to go. Everyone seems to know what they need to do. Breakfast is not a high priority, (I'm not including coffee in that statement – that's why we brought our Keurig, which Carrie was equally glad to use that morning).

We did snack on fruit and such, unintentionally laid out on the picnic table. For Amy and I , we did not have that much to do to be ready and gone, but we stayed with Nate and Carrie as he tightly and efficiently packed the back of his truck. Not much room left after he Tetris'd everything.

As I mentioned earlier in this book, I had received a box from my brother Jay, of mementos from my mum who'd passed away in April last year. He'd had it quite some months. His wife Jenn knew where to retrieve it. The main prize for me was the family Bible – a large, red, very fancy coffee table book that had adorned my life growing up. I'd loved looking at the many pictures – religious paintings from masters of centuries past. Printed around 1954, it now showed its age.

The box also had some books, some statues and a large envelope with photographs. My favorite of those pics - my high school senior picture. For reasons unknown, St. Joseph High School in Ogden had opted for black and white senior pictures that year. It still looks wonderful. I am not particularly photogenic, but that picture is one of my favorites.

The box also held a few books mum sent to my daughter, Steven, in Bellingham, WA., which to this day I have not yet seen her to pass along.
As we were packing up, I hauled out the box from the RV basement storage aboard Morris to show to Carrie and Nate. Very fun treasures.

Check out time is 11 a.m. To my surprise, by time we got everything stowed to travel, including the electric cables and water, it was a quarter to eleven. I also failed to mention that the House Batteries were not charging properly. Probably the power converter, which I would try to change after we got home. It could also be a failed battery cable. I did not bring my electrical tester, but I did bring my battery charger, so kept the batteries fully charged so we'd have lights at night. More to put away in the morning.

Carrie and Nate left around 10:30, heading home to Omaha. We said our good-byes like everyone does. It's always a blessing to see them as well, even if we're also glad to be on our way. The length of the camping trip was neither too short nor too long.

As you already know, traveling in an RV, one must make sure everything is stowed properly before we ventured out. Assured all was stowed to travel, we headed forward out of our campsite, turning to the left to make our final trek through the park. Immediately, we heard a small crash in the cabin. Looking back, the fridge door had flown open, and some items fell out, including the eggs. Four of them broke on the rug.

I stopped and Amy went back to clean up. We figured Emi did not close the door tightly, but really, it could have been any of us.

We sat there in the road for the 10-minutes it took for Amy to clean up the spills and replace items in the fridge. Fortunately, we blocked no one trying to get through.

While waiting, suddenly Carrie and Nate came up behind us. They'd forgotten to give Amy something from her brother, so were doubly glad that we had not yet left.

Just as remarkable, they told us the next campers had already occupied our campsite. We'd not been gone even ten minutes. Impressive!
Sharing hugs and good-byes again, we continued our exit, first stopping at the RV dump to empty things out. I'm sure you don't want details.

We had a bunch of hours of driving ahead of us, heading west towards home. Like in Amy & Dave's COVID Escape Tour - 2021, we winged it; playing it by ear to decide where to camp for the night. I was tempted to just drive late into the night to home, but the passenger headlight is touchy and sometimes goes off. I have cleaned the contacts and used a wad of duct tape to create pressure against one side so it will remain lit. It works pretty well, but certainly not perfect.

Also, my brother Jay had been hired for another driving job, but Jenn still drove down to Spokane to meet us for Mexican dinner. We returned the solar panel and extra propane tank. The dinnertime was delightful. No hurry at all. She's such a blessed person to have in our lives.
Likewise, we were not in a big hurry to get home, even if we did miss our doggies. Looking ahead on Amy's phone, we found a campsite by a lake in

Sprague, WA, about 35 miles past Spokane. That would be our target camping for the night.

The town is kind of half Mayberry and half Great Depression. Amy joked that we might not get out of there with our lives.

We stopped at the small grocery store for ice and a couple more snacks we did not need for the evening and the drive home. We had PLENTY of food from our travels – leftovers from our regular dining out and such. We would feast on whatever we wanted after we set up camp.

The campsite is actually just a basic, open parking space, but still kind of nice. Sprague Lake is a long drink of water. The campsites are at the eastern end. You can see I-90 from there. There are a couple short piers heading out over the water. A portly man in a too tight red T-shirt sat fishing in a very small dingy. The water was completely calm – a blessing for him, I'm sure, since it looked like it would not take much to tip over.

I strolled out onto the pier and took some pics with my fancy Nikon. Nothing to write home about, but still a nice time. It has an amazing zoom – fun to play with.

We opted to pull out our fire pit and propane to set-up by the water. A couple camp chairs. My guitar. What else could be more perfect? Easy answer. No mosquitoes. As soon as the sun dropped behind the hill, they came out in droves. We had to flee back to Morris. I put the pit, tank and chairs away in record time. Even after we got inside, still a bit pre-twilight, we could see the mosquitoes trying to get inside against the screens and windows.

Whatever. We were safe and only had to kill a couple of the bloodsuckers that had followed us in.

As much as we enjoyed our time with Carrie, Nate and Emi, it was also nice to have our little home-away-from-home solely ours again. We watched some YouTube videos on our phones and snacked on the items we still should not have bought in town. The ceiling lights stayed bright for the duration of the evening.

Amy settled into bed for the night. I spent the last hour or so typing on this book.

Visiting with Jennifer who met us in Spokane

Sprague Lake Campground For the Night

Friday, July 18, 2025
Final Drive Home

We wanted to get home, but felt no urgency to hit the road as early as possible. I knew the bloodsuckers would still be outside in great number. Waiting until the sun was high in the sky seemed prudent.

We doddled around Morris for the first hour of the morning, making coffee and enjoying the lull of the new day as we let our minds and souls awaken.

I enjoy Bible reading in the morning with my coffee. On these trips, my reading becomes less ritual and thereby, more haphazard. Though there certainly is plenty of room for a large book in a motorhome, I typically leave my NIV Study Bible at home. I have a few Bible versions in my phone I can read. They work fine, but one cannot underline words or jot ideas as easily.

Sprague is 346 miles from Sequim. Officially 5 hours and 38 minutes, according to GPS. Plenty of time to get home that day if nothing bad happened. Morris never travels as fast as the GPS advises.

The only outside connection I'd made was the electricity. I ran out, unplugged and stowed the cable. A few determined mosquitoes still tried to make acquaintances. We parted company quickly.

Safe back inside. We headed out. About half the campers had already left, and I expect some of the others were staying longer. Again - nothing fancy about this place, but during the day, it could be a very pleasant camping nook.

Instead of heading back through town, I turned to the west to follow the long, narrow lake. The sun behind us. A patchy country road ahead. Very sweet.

Past the lake, easy access to I-90.

We crossed the "Great Plains" of Eastern Washington without incidence. Moderate, summertime traffic.

Some miles past Ellensburg, the terrain changes dramatically. First some rolling hills. Those huge, white windmills are switched out for real trees which become thicker and more plentiful as we traverse further west. The hills turn into mountains with sizable passes. Morris likes to take his time checking out the sites as we climb over the passes.

A couple hours plus down the road, Amy wanted breakfast. Nowadays, we are so blessed with our cell phones in many ways. Amy found a small breakfast place in Cle Elum, WA with Gluten Free options.

I always liked the name Cle Elum. It's certainly unique. Cle Elum means "Swift Water" in the Kittitas tribal language, referring to the nearby Cle Elum river.

I have to share this silly story that occurred a few years back.

At church one evening, doing Bible study with Pastor Jerry and a few other men, PJ (my nickname for Pastor Jerry) shared updates about his aging father. Deep into dementia, Jerry would talk about some of their conversations, the ways he had to oversee and even police the quality of care he received, and so on.

PJ said his father was trying to remember the name of a city for some account he wanted to recite. Jerry named a few cities without success. His only clue – the name of the city began with the letter M. They never figured out the town name.
Us men around the table took to task, offering names of cities in the area that began with M.

PJ's dad, (who was also named Jerry), lived most of his life in western Oregon, so PJ figured it was an Oregon city.

Medford?

Nope.

Milwaukie?

Nope.

McMinnville?

Nope.

So, PJ tried Washington State cities that began with M.

Mill Creek?

Nope.

Mukiteo?

Nope.

Marysville?

Nope.

Mount Vernon?

Nope.

Suddenly, I suggested "Mule Elk?"

Lots of blank stares from that one. I added, "That's Cle Elum spelled backwards. Mule Elc."

Groans abounded. Let us continue.

Cle Elum streets are not the best for driving a large motorhome, but not like trying to navigate through a big city like Seattle. Amy gave directions to the small breakfast place. I was able to park in an actual parking lot with sufficient room to maneuver when time to leave. A short walk to the café – one of many small businesses along this large building that seemed like it should not have many patrons, but apparently many of the locals went there regularly.

We ordered coffee and breakfast. I got a fancy, dressed and toasted bagel. Amy got eggs. We enjoyed our breakfast there rather than try to drive and eat, which honestly is not that hard in a big, lumbering RV.

The GPS said a few hours further to home, but we would be hitting Seattle-Tacoma I-5 around rush hour. I mentally prepared to relax and mosey along the freeway until we got home.

RV's and motorpool diamond lanes are not usually good matches. I prefer it when I'm driving a smaller vehicle. Morris pisses off lots of travelers, so I just stayed in the right lane traffic and took our time getting home. Still plenty of hours before dark.

One significant thought occurred to both of us on this trip. We bought Morris in 2021. It has the same tires. It sat in a back yard field for some years before we bought it. I have no idea how old the tires are. Likely ten to fifteen years old, if not older.

In 2021, the age of the tires never crossed my mind that I recall. This time, I thought about it a lot, especially concerned if one of the front tires popped. That did not happen, (thank You, Jesus), but we considered, if we're going to keep Morris, we probably better get him new tires.

Continuing our final trek, I would love to say that we witnessed a terrible accident and had to jump out to render first aid, carrying the half-dead corpse into our RV to get them medical help, but sadly, nothing so dire or terrible happened to make this last chapter more interesting. Actually, I'm more than glad we never encountered any such danger.

We left I-5 in Tacoma, turning onto Highway 16 towards the Tacoma Narrows Bridge, Gig Harbor, Port Orchard and another hour and a half to home.

Shelby was there when we arrived. Our doggies, Toby and Cricket were more than glad to see us again. They cannot contain their excitement within their skins when we just go shopping. Being gone all those days just adds all that much more to their ecstasy to see us again.

We shared our adventures with Shelby and her dog, Loki. We thanked her and paid her and were more than glad to be home again. I unpacked a few items, but most would be glad to hang out in

Morris until tomorrow. Just plug in the electricity and the fridge will do its job for another day.

And with no further ado, that was our trip to Fruitland, WA and Glacier National Park.

* Many Thanks to you for sharing time with me. Your Reviews are greatly appreciated. Feedback also always welcome.
May God's blessings be ever with you in your walk with Jesus and His Holy Spirit.

If you like the book,
please review it.
It's very helpful for letting
others know about it.

Other Books by David Stoeckl

- Patmos – An Apostle in Exile – A Planet on Trial (a Historic, Biblical Novel)
- Patmos is also available as an Audiobook
- Life's Vagabondage (an Allegorical Novel)
- Life's Vagabondage Audiobook (Coming Soon)
- Tossing Mountains – Where are the Miracles Today Like We Read About in the Bible?
- Silhouette of God – A Bit of Poetry
- Oops! There Goes Another One (a Novel)
- Julesburg Cruisin' Night (a Pictorial)
- An Awful Lot Like Me (a Novella)
- Amy and Dave's COVID Escape Tour – 2021
- Amy and Dave's Portugal Escape Tour – 2023
- Your Quick Guide to Understanding Subsidized Housing (How to apply for HUD Housing)
- His Heart Art – a Devotional
- 52 Diets a Year (Pen Name David Sterling)
- 40 Days Christian Devotional (Pending)
- 5 Minute Readings (ie, Fun Short Stories)

(& More To Come)

www.ingramcontent.com/pod-product-compliance
Lightning Source LLC
LaVergne TN
LVHW091302080426
835510LV00007B/364